# BLADEN COUNTY, NORTH CAROLINA ABSTRACTS OF EARLY DEEDS
## 1738 - 1804

by:
Brent H. Holcomb, C. A. L. S.

Southern Historical Press, Inc.
Greenville, South Carolina

Copyright 1979
By: Southern Historical Press, Inc.

All rights reserved. No part of this publication may be reproduced, stored in a retrieval system, transmitted in any form, posted on to the web in any form or by any means without the prior written permission of the publisher.

Please direct all correspondence and orders to:

www.southernhistoricalpress.com
or
**SOUTHERN HISTORICAL PRESS, Inc.
PO BOX 1267
375 West Broad Street
Greenville, SC 29601
southernhistoricalpress@gmail.com**

ISBN #0-89308-189-2

*Printed in the United States of America*

INTRODUCTION

    The early period which these deeds cover expresses the importance of them. Unfortunately, many Bladen deeds were lost in the three court house fires. The two volumes abstracted here seem to be made up from the remnants of deed books or loose deeds in the court house. There may be some deed books in Elizabethtown or in the N. C. Archives which overlap the latter period of these abstracts (1787-1804).

    At its formation in 1734 Bladen encompassed everything west of the present county. There were several border changes between Cumberland and Bladen County, as well as the fact that Cumberland County was formed totally out of Bladen, and part of Orange County came from it as well. Anson County was carved out of Bladen 1748 or 1749, and Robeson County in 1787.

    The abstracts contained in this volume are especially informative, with many long chains of title going back to original grants, and many references to bordering Craven County, South Carolina. This book will provide many links which were formerly thought forever lost.

                                              Brent H. Holcomb, C. A. L. S.
                                              Columbia, S. C.
                                              August 29, 1979

1738-1779

Page 1: N. C., Bladen County, 18 Dec 1778, Thomas Amis of the
County and State of North Carolina, to Dempsey Dawson of
same, for Ł 30 proc. money...42 A, part of 50 A on E side Drownd-
ing Creek on S side Cabbage Swamp, adj. William Stricklins line,
formerly Gideon Tilmans line, granted to said Thomas Amis by pa-
tent 22 Jan 1773, also part of a tract of land 33 A which Thomas
Amis purchased of William Stricklan Senr by deed 2 Nov 1773...
Thomas Amis (Seal), Wit: John Colman, Stephen Barfield, William
Stricklin. Feby Term 1779. Prov. by John Colman. ·John White,
C. C.

Page 2: 6 May 1778, James Sattar & wife Sarah of Bladen Co., to
Alexander Bradie of same, for Ł 10 current money of NC
...lot of land in Elizabethtown ½ A, and numbered 115...James
Saltar (Seal), Sarah Saltar (Seal), Wit: Archcd. Darrah, Alexr.
Harvey. Bladen May 1778, This deed was acknowledged in open
court and ordered to be registered.

Pp. 2-3: 9 Oct 1773, Walter Gibson, William Saltor, James White,
James Bailey and Benjamin Humphreys, Directors of the
Town of Elizabeth, to Benjamin Fitzrandolph of Bladen County,
for Ł 2 proc. money ½ A lot in Elizabethtown, # 99...William
Saltor (Seal), James Bailey (Seal), Benjamin Humphreys (Seal),
Wit: John White, David Russ. Bladen May 1775, This deed was
proved by the oath of David Russ and ordered Registered. A.
Moore Clk.

Pp. 3-4: 4 Aug 1777, Christopher Sanders & wife Sarah of Bladen
County, to Daniel Shipman of same, for Ł 20 proc. money
...land on a branch of the Western prong of the wakamaw being
a part of a tract of 444 A adj. Adams line, Thomas Robesons line,
line that was Thomas Robesons now the said Christopher Sanders,
the said Daniel to have 40 A, adj. Thomas Robinson, David Clark,
Joshua Hayses line...Christopher Sanders (X) (Seal), Sarah
Sanders (X) (Seal), Wit: James Shipman, Matthew Kelly. August
Term 1777. Prov. by James Shipman. John White, C. C.

Pp. 4-5: 4 Aug 1777, Christopher Sanders & wife Sarah to Daniel
Shipman, for Ł 60 proc. money...land on a branch of
the Western prong of the wakamaw, 150 A, granted to Henry Sims,
of which Thomas Robeson became lawfully Seized and possessed of
and conveyed the same to David Clark, and the said David Clark by
virtue of the same to William Sanders, and by the death of the
said William Sanders the above named Christopher Sanders became
the lawful heir and owner of said land...Christopher Sanders (X)
(Seal), Sarah Sanders (X) (Seal), Wit: James Shipman, Matthew
Kelly. August Term 1777. Proved in open court by James Shipman.

Page 5: Thomas Sanders Will. I, Thomas Sanders of Bladen County
for love and affection...my beloved wife Emilia Sanders
all my real and personal Estate during her life time is She sur-
vives me...with the condition of her paying one shilling sterling
to each of these our children they having received their full
proportion of the house heretofore viz Elizabeth Boswell, Elizabeth Ellis, Amili Morley, Thomas Browder and Elcy Sanders, my
daughter in law...16 Nov 1776...Thomas Sanders (Seal), Wit:
Duncan Morrison & Sinrill Hardwick. Prov. by Duncan Morrison.
John White, C. C.

Pp. 6-9: This Indenture Tripartie 10 April 1755, between John

1

1738-1779

Burgwin of Wilmington, New Hanover County, Merchant and Margaret his wife one of the daughters and CoHeirs unto Rodger Haynes, late of the County aforesaid, Gentleman, deceased, of the first part, Mary Haynes the other daughter coheir unto the said Roger Haynes of the second part and Margaret Haynes of the County and Province aforesaid widow and Relict of the said Rodger of the third part...Roger Haynes in his life time was seized of three several plantations tracts or parcels of land; one tract containing 1000 acres in the County aforesaid between Prince Georges and the North East Branch of Cape Fear River, adj. Andrew Legers lower line; 640 A in Bladen County on the Western side of the White Marsh adj. the land on which Edmond Rock now lives, purchased by said Rodger Haynes from Samuel and Joseph Portexsent; 666 2/3 acres in New Hanover County between Prince Georges Creek and the North East branch of Cape Fear River adj. lands formerly belonging to John Marshal and the Rev. Dr. Richard Marsden, Andrew Legere....J Burgwin (Seal), Margaret Burgwin (Seal), Mary Haynes (Seal), Margt. Haynes (Seal), Wit: Francis Bull, John Gardner. Prov. by John Gardner 31 Aug 1756. Peter Henly, C. J. Registered in Book D, folio 293 p James Macon Regr. Registered in the Registers office of Bladen County in Book E, folio 187.

Pp. 9-10: 13 Aug 1767, John Dubois of Wilmington, Esquire, & wife Jane, to John Jones of Duplin County, Merchent, for Ł 300 proc. money, 584 acres, part of 600 acres granted by King George II to John Clayton 19 May 1735, and the said 584 acres conveyed by said John Clayton by assignment indorsed on the said patent bearing date 12 Aug 1736 to the said John Dubois ...Jno. Du Bois (Seal), Jane Dubois (Seal), Wit: A. MacLaine. Wilmington 9th Dec 1768, prov. by Archibal MacLain, and Jane Dubois relinquished dower without the compulsion of her late husband the said John Dubois.

Page 11: N. C., Bladen County: John White of the County aforesd., & wife Mary for love, good will and affection to our beloved son in law Alexander Harvey of ye same place (cordwainer) land on NE side of the NW branch of Cape Fear River, adj. Joseph Kemp, 190 A...3 May 1768...John White (Seal), Mary White (Seal), Wit: William White, Robt White. Prov. by Robert White, Bladen May Court 1768. Arthur Howe, Ck. Ct.

Pp. 11-12: N. C., Bladen County: John White & wife Mary to son in law Joseph Kemp of same place (cooper)...land on NE side NW branch of Cape Fear River, 203 A...John White (Seal) Mary White (Seal), Wit: Robert Edwards, James White. dated 1759. Prov. by Robert Edwards, April Court 1759, Bladen County. J. Burgwin, C. Registered in the Registers office in Bladen County Book E, fo. 84. J. Burgwin, Regr.

Pp. 12-13: N. C., Bladen County: John White & wife Mary to daughter Jane Kemp (alias White), negro Bess near four years of age...4 Apr 1759...John White (Seal), Wit: Robert Edwards, James White. Prov. by Robert Edwards, April Court 1759. J. Burgwin, Regr.

Pp. 13-14: 22 Aug 1765, Robert Johnson Esquire Sheriff of Bladen County, to John Burgwin of Wilmington, Esqr., ...by a writ of Fiera facias issuing out of the Superior Court of Justice at Wilmington on 15 Oct 1765, to sell the goods, etc. of Henry Boswell and James Baley Ł 42 s 15 proc. money...recovered by Robert Cochran and Ann his wife Extrx and John Robeson Exr. of the last will and testament of John Nessfield deceased...land adj.

1738-1779

upper part of Hail Park plantation 100 A, formerly property of
John Nesfield, whereon the said Henry Baswell now lives...for Ł
22 proc. money....Robert Johnson Shff (Seal), Wit: Arthur Council,
James Bailey. June 1, 1769, proved by James Bailey. M. Howard,
C. J.

Pp. 15-16: 4 Apr 1761, Alexander McKay & wife Jane of Bladen Co.,
to John Boyd of same, Cordewindix (sic) for Ł 30 proc.
money...land on SW side of the North West River on the lower
side of Hammonds Creek, part of 100 A formerly the property of
Maurice Moore Esqr., and conveyed to McKay, adj. to land surveyed
to Samuel Pike, Neill McKay, C. Boyd, 250 A, part of 1000 A (a-
nother tract?)...Alexander McKay (Seal), Jane McKay (X) (Seal),
Wit: Richard Mullington, Thomas White. Prov. in Bladen County
May Court 1761, ack. by Alexander McKay. Registered in the Registers office of Bladen County, in Book E, fol. 147.

Pp. 16-18: 2 May 1768, Robert Johnson Esqr Sheriff of Bladen Co.,
to John Burgwin of Wilmington Esqr. by a writ of Fi
Fa from the district of Wilmington, 27 Nov 1768 (sic), against
the goods etc. of Thomas Evans, recovered by James Bailey & Co
...land on NE side of the North West River opposite to Hail Park
and between lands formerly of John Protrough and Griffith Jones,
granted by Patent to Peter Evans and conveyed to sd. Thomas Evans
...Robert Johnson (Seal), Wit: James Bailey, Arthur Council.
Prov. June 1, 1769, by James Bailey. Martin Howard, C. J.

Pp. 19-20: 16 Aug 1767, Jeremiah Plummer of Bladen County, planter
& wife Sarah to James Bailey & Co., Merchants of same,
for Ł 60 proc. money...a piece of land, one moity, which was
bequeathed per deed of gift in the lifetime of Joseph and Ellipha
Plummer by them to Jeremiah and Joseph Plummer, by deed registered
in the office of said county in Book b, page 242, 19 March 1746
150 A...Jeremiah Plummer (Seal), Sarah Plummer (X) (Seal), Wit:
David Morley, Peter Lord. Bladen, August Term 1757, prov. by David Morley. Arthur Howe, Clerk.

Pp. 20-21: James Stewart of Bladen County, NC, planter, for Ł 20
proc. money pd. by Neil McNeil of Cumberland County,
planter...on west side of Raft Swamp, 100 A, a tract of land
granted to William Carver, 3 March 1755, and by deed from sd.
Carver to said Stewart...11 Oct 1768...James Stewart (I) (Seal),
Wit: Joseph Fort, Jesse Bagget. Bladen, Novr. Court 1768, Prov.
by Jos. Fort, and ordered to be registered. A. Howe, Clerk.

Pp. 21-22: N. C. Bladen County: Meriday Ellzey of county aforesd.,
for Ł 80 proc. money to Elish Sweeting of Anson Co.,
100 A on Shoe Heel in a pond below the plantation....10 March
1769...Meriday Elbzey (M) (Seal), Wit: Richd Smith, Jacob Alford.
Bladen May Court 1769. Prov. by Richard Smith, A. Howe, Clr. Cor.

Pp. 22-23: Solomon James Senr., of Bladen County, for Ł 20 proc.
money to Richard Smith, 100 A on NE side of Drowning
Creek on the back side of the Road a little below the said Smith's
bridge...10 March 1769...Solmon James Senr (Seal), Wit: John
Blount, Philip Blount (X). Bladen, May Court 1769. Ack by Solomon
James. A Howe, Clr. Cot.

Pp. 24-26: 25 May 1757, George Ronald of Glasgoa in North Brittain,
Merchant, who was surviving copartner of Charles Hepburn, both State of Brunswick on Capefear River in North Carolina

by John Starkey and John Clitheral his attorneys to John Smith of Bladen Co., planter, for Ł 40 proc. money...land on NE side of NW branch of the Capefear River, land granted to Richard Singletary by Gabriel Johnston Esqr., 19 June 1736, and con to sd. George Ronald and Charles Hepburn by deed 26 Feb 1738... George Ronald (Seal), Wit: Jos Burgwin, Willm Bartram. By power of attorney John Starkey and John Clitherall, dated 18 Apr 1751. Prov. by William Bartram Oct. 1757. Registered in the Registers office of Bladen County in Book E, F. 24.

Pp. 26-27: 16 January 1769, John Rowan of Brunswick Co., to Richard Saltar of Bladen Co., planter, for Ł 200 proc. money...land on NE side Northwest River adj. Edmond Chancey, Judge Leonard, 640 A, granted 16 Apr 1765 to sd. Rowan...John Rowan, Wit: Robert Stewart, Dennis Lennon. Bladen, Feby Court 1769. Prov. by Dennis Lennon, A. Howe., Clr. Cor.

Pp. 28-29: 26 Apr 1756, George Thomas of Bladen Co., planter, & wife Jane to John Boyd of same, Cordwinder, for Ł 30 proc. money...134 A on E side Northwest River, part of 575 A granted by Arthur Dobbs Gov. &C. to sd. George Thomas and formerly known as Streets or Pucketts Land, adj. Daniel Melvin...George Thomas (E) (Seal), Jane Thomas (Seal), Wit: Daniel Melvin, Richard Singletary. 5th Feby 1772, Bladen County Court, prov. by Richard Singletary.
Acknowledged April Court 1756 E. H. D. Matanwe Colill(?) C. C.

Pp. 29-30: Thomas Davis late of South Carolina, Planter, for Ł 25 proc. money to John Fiverash, planter of Bladen Co., N. C., unto John Fivash, land on S side Wilkesons Swamp, adj. James Wilkerson, 200 A granted to William Wilkerson 22 Dec 1763...5 Nov 1767. Thomas Davis (X) (Seal), Wit: Abraham Barnes, Donald McLean. Bladen May Court 1768, prov. by Abraham Barnes. Arthur Howe, Clr. Cor.

Pp. 30-31: Andrew Graham of Bladen Co., Ship Carpenter, for Ł 2 proc. money to Benjamin Clark of same, planter, 81½A on NE side of the N. W. River, part of a pattent to said Andrew Graham...7 May 1767...Andrew Graham (Seal), Wit: Robert Edwards, John Beard. Bladen, August Court 1768, Prov. by Robert Edwards. A. Howe.

Pp. 32-33: 16 Oct 1769, Richard Chessen of Angelo County, N. C. to John Campbell of Bladen Co., for Ł 8 s 10 proc. money...land on branches of Carvers Creek, adj. Charles Benbo, Samuel Pike...Richard Cheasten (Seal), Wit: George Keller, Robert Bercy. Prov. by George Kelling, 29 Dec 1769. M. Moore.

Pp. 33-34: N. C. Bladen County: Stephen Hollingsworth, Miller, & wife Mary to Neill Beard, planter, for Ł 300...land on NE side of NW River adj. sd. Stephen Hollingsworth, Robert Edwards, 250 A granted to sd. Hollingsworth....25 Jan 1755/6... Stephen Hollingsworth (Seal), Mary Hollingsworth (Seal), Wit: Vallentine Hollingsworth, Archibald McClaren ( ). Prov. in open court Sept 1746 by Vallentine Hollingsworth. Thos Robeson, C. C. Registered in the registers office of Bladen County in Book B, Folio 191, Oct 5th, 1746. Thos Robeson Regr.

Pp. 34-35: Robert Edwards Planter to Neill Beard planter, for Ł 26 s 13 d 4 proc. money...125 A on NE side on the NW river joining the lands of the said Stephen Hollingsworth, Robert Edwards; equally to divide a tract of land containing 250 A granted to sd. Hollingsworth...25 Jan 1756...Stephen Hollingsworth (Seal), Mary Hollingsworth (Seal), Wit: Vallentin Hollingsworth, Archibald Mcclaren ( ). Proved in open Court Sept. 1746 by the oath of Vallentine Hollingsworth. Thos Robeson, C. C. Registered in the registers office of Bladen County in Book B, Folio 191, Octr. 5th 1846. Thos. Robeson, Regr.

Pp. 34-35: N. C. Bladen County, Robert Edwards, planter, to Neill Beard, planter, both of Co. aforesd., for Ł 76 s 13 d 4 proc. money...125 A on NE side of the North West branch of Cape Fear, the moiety of a tract granted to Stephen Hollingsworth adj. John Gervis...13 June 1752...Robert Edwards (Seal), Wit: Robert Dionery, Alexdr. McConley. Ack. in open court June 1752 by Robert Edwards. Registered in the Registers office of Bladen County, N. C., in Book D, folio no. 33, June 16th, 1752. Thos Roberson, Regr.

Pp. 35-37: 24 Feb 1769, Richard Barefield of South Carolina, planter, to John Smith, Orange County, N. C., planter, ...Richard Barefield and wife Mary, for Ł 70 proc. money...land in Bladen County in the fork between Ashpole & Hogg Swamp, patent dated 1 July 1758, 200 A...Richard Barefield (R), Mary Barefield (N), Wit: Danl Willis, Joshua Barefield. May Court 1770, prov. by Daniel Willis, Martin Colville, C. C.

Pp. 37-38: 12 June 1769, Joshua Lamb of South Carolina, planter, to John Smith late of Bladen County, planter, for Ł 15 proc. money...100 A in Bladen County on S side Drowning Creek in the fork between Ashpole & Indian Swamp, granted 20 Oct 1758 ....Joshua Lamb (Seal), Wit: Danl Willis, Christopher Garlington. May Court 1770, prov. by Daniel Willis, Maturin Colville, C. C.

Pp. 39-40: North Carolina: 18 Oct 1769, Brinkley Corbett of Bladen Co., planter, to Abel Corbett, planter of same, for Ł 20 proc. money...land on SW side of the North West River of Cape Fear the Middle Marsh of Swanns Creek including Michael Odom's improvements...Brinkley Corbett (Seal), Wit: William Johnson, Samuel Bel nnad(?). May Court 1770, prov. by William Johnson. Maturin Colvell, C. C.

Pp. 40-41: Richard Mullington of Bladen County for love, good will and affection to my grandson Josiah Lewis Junr, land in Bladen County on the SW side of the Brown Marsh Swamp, 100 A, being the lower part of a tract of 200 A granted to me by Gabriel Johnston, Esqr Gov. dated 8 June 1739...Richard Mullington (Seal), Wit: Thomas Singletary, George Rowan. May Court 1770. Ack. in open court by Mullington. Maturin Colvell, C. C. Dated 10 June 1769.

Pp. 41-42: William How of Bladen County, N. C., for love, good will and affection to my grandson William Holmes, 50 A in Bladen County, part of 200 A on Hammonds Creek granted by Gov. Gabriel Johnston to Thomas White, late of the aforesaid county, decd., 21 Oct 1758, and by deed from Thomas White to William How 27 Jan 1760...3 Oct 1769...Wm How (X) (Seal), Wit: Robert Berry, Richd. Mullington. May court 1770, prov. by Richard Mullington, Maturin Colvill, C. C.

Pp. 42-43: 19 Oct 1767, Samuel Pike of Bladen County, N. C., planter, to Jonadab Russ of same, planter, for Ł 25 proc.

money....land in Bladen County on Carvers Creek 150 A granted by Mat Rowan, to Samuel Pike 5 Feb 1754, adj. Gershom Benbow, Charles Benbow, 150 A...Samuel Pike (Seal), Wit: Stephen Shepperd, Aless Trueblood. May Court 1770, prov. by Stephen Shepperd. Maturin Colvill, C. C.

Pp. 44-45: 13 Mar 1770, Dennis Lennon of Bladen Co., Inkeeper, & wife Experience to Thomas Browder of same, planter, for Ŀ 33 proc. money...land on SW side of White Oak Branch of Waggamaw Swamp adj. Mathew Rowan, 400 A...Dennis Lennon (Seal), Experience Lennon (Seal), Wit: Jas White, James Salter. May Court 1770, Ack. in open court. Maturin Colvill, C. C.

Pp. 45-46: 10 Mar 1770, James Inman, planter, of Bladen Co., NC, & wife Elizabeth, to Stephen Flear, planter, for Ŀ 18 proc. money...land on the head of Indian Swamp, where the sd. Glear now lives, down the branch to the mouth of a small branch where William Barrot formerly cleared, 300 A adj. Edward Flowers, pattd. by sd. Inman...James Inman (I) (Seal), Elizabeth Inman (X) (Seal), Wit: Danl. Willis, Rodger Bearfield. May Court 1770, prov. by the oath of Daniel Willis. Maturin Colvell, C. C.

Pp. 47-48: Daniel Melvin of Bladen County, planter, for Ŀ 40 proc. money, pd. by John Sikes of same, cooper... land on SW side of South River between Mausdons and Joseph Locks land, 150 A...Danl. Melvin (Seal), Wit: Mathew Garvan, Jacob Sikes. May Court 1770, Prov. by Daniel Melvin. Maturin Colvell, C. C.

Pp. 48-50: 30 Apr 1770, James Blount, planter, of South Carolina, to Roger Barrfield, planter, of Bladen Co., ...said James Blount & wife Sarah...for Ŀ 40 proc. money...300 A adj. Flowers Swamp, west of Drowning Creek...granted by pattent 3 May 1769...James Blount (J) (Seal), Sarah Blount (+) (Seal), Wit: Danl. Willis, Joel Pitman. May Court 1770, Prov. by Daniel Willis. Maturin Colvill, C. C.

Pp. 50-51: N. C., Bladen County: Joseph Cooper & wife Mary of county aforesd., for Ŀ 200 proc. money to Jesse Newbery of same, 653 A, part of three surveys for different pattents on SW side of the North West Branch of Capefear River, 640 A pattented by James McDaniel 16 Nov 1764; 225 A pattented by William Gray 350 A 10 Sept 1735, rec. inthe Secretarys in Book No. 7, page 93; land heretofore given by James McDaniel in Exchange to said Jesse Cooper for a parcel on the other side of the River opposite thereunto...24 Feb 1765. Jesse Cooper (Seal), Mary Cooper (Seal), Wit: Ro. Edwards, John McMath. May Court 1765, ack. in open court by Joseph Cooper. Registered in the registers office in Book E, Folio 315.

Pp. 51-53: N. C., Bladen County, John Newburry Junr, Wheelright, and wife Mary of same, for Ŀ 330...½ of a tract to Jesse Newburry, on Espie's Creek, near west of Cooper's saw & grist mill, 160 A part of James McDaniel's lower pattented land and partly out of a pattent granted William Gray Junr... John Newburry (Seal), Mary Newburry (X) (Seal), Wit: Joseph Thembe (X), John Ligett. Dated 1 Nov 1768. Bladen Novr Court 1768, ack. by John Newburry and Mary his wife... Arthur How, Clk Cur.

1738-1779

Pp. 53-54: N. C., Bladen County: Joseph and Mary Cooper (later says Jesse and Mary Cooper), for Ł 100 to Jesse Newburry...land on SW side of the N. W. River about half a mile above the mouth of Elpie's Creek adj. John Newberry, where Joseph Thombs's saw and grist mill now stands, part pattented to William Gray and part by Neill Gray 1735...Joseph Cooper (Seal), Mary Cooper (Seal), Wit: Joseph Shembs (+), John Legett. dated 1 Nov 1768. Novr Court 1768, Ack. by Joseph Cooper and wife. A. Hows, Clr Cor.

Pp. 55-56: N. C. Bladen County, Joseph Cooper & wife Mary to Jesse Newberry for Ł 5 s 5 proc. money...land on SW side of the NW branch of Capefear River, the moiety of a tract granted by Gov. Dobbs 1764, Rec. in Secretary's office in Book No. 12, page 85...Joseph Cooper (Seal), Mary Cooper (Seal), Wit: Robt Edwards, John McMath. dated 24 Feb 1765. May Court 1765, ack. by Joseph Cooper. Registered in Book __ Folio 213. Maturin Colvell, Regr.

Pp. 56-58: 13 Sept 1764, Joseph Cooper of Bladen Co., to Jesse Newberry, milright, of same, for Ł 80 proc. money... 220 A part of a piece of land which in William Grays last Division he gave to his Daughter Agniss, wife of James McDaniel, and part thereof was granted to said Gray 10 Sept 1735, and part was granted to ____ ...Joseph Cooper (Seal), Mary Cooper (Seal), Wit: Wm Maulsby, John McMath, Benjn Cooper. May Court 1765, ack. by Joseph Ceoper. Maturin Colvill, C. C. Registered in Book E, folio 308.

Pp. 58-60: 17 Oct 1763, Joseph Cooper of Bladen Co., planter, & wife Mary, to James McDaniel, planter, (consideration not given)...land on NE side of the N. West River of the Capefear ...to the Stone Quarey, adj. William Gray, Winnings, Mary Gray, opposite to Chanceys House, a part of the land of William Gray deceased which in his last division he appointed for his daughter Agniss Gray wife of the said James McDaniel...apparently an exchange of land....Joseph Cooper (Seal), Mary Cooper (Seal), Wit: George Cooper, Benjn Cooper. May Court 1770, ack. in open court by Joseph Cooper, Registered in Book E, folio 306. Maturin Colvill, Register.

Pp. 60-62: Article of agreement 3 Oct 1758, between William Gray of Bladen County, planter, and Andrew Graham his Cousin of same...the above named William Gray doth lease unto the above named Andrew Graham during his Natural life, land on W side of the NW River in Bladen County, being the lower part of land pattented in his sons name Neill Gray deceased, being the property of Margaret Gray his Daughter, 150 A, granting the priviledge of build two Saw Mills on the Creek in partnership with Gray Graham...then to make the following division: Margaret Grays part is on the East side of the North West River adj. Andrew Grahams upper line....Mary Grays on the west side of the River...Agness Grays part now the wife of James McDaniel from Mary Grays upper line...Elizabeth Grays part from Agness Grays upper line excepting what is given by deed to Mr. William McKinzie in the hands of Captain Quince out of Elizabeth part...Will: Gray (Seal), Andrew Graham (Seal), Wit: John Chandler(Ŧ), James McDaniel. Bladen County, Oct. Court 1759. Prov. by James McDaniel and recorded in the minutes of said Court. Registered in Book E, folio 97. John Burgwin, Regr.

Pp. 62-63: 8 May 1741, John Sinscom of Newhanover County, N. C.
to Stephen Hollingsworth of Bladen County, for ₤ 80
...land in the county of Bladen, 300 A, on NE side of the NW River
adj. Richard Davis...John Linscom (Seal), Wit: Edwd. Harrison,
Will Gray. Deed Registered June 23rd 1741 in Bladen Book folio
230 Pr John Clayton, Regr.

Pp. 64-65: North Carolina, Bladen Precinct, Richard Dunn, Blacksmith, of Precint and Prov. aforesd., to Stephen
Hollingsworth, Cordwinder of same, Richd. Dunn & wife Elizabeth,
for ₤ 100...150 A on NE side of the North West River adj. said
Stephen Hollingsworth, John Linscom...13 Dec 1750. Richd Dunn
(Seal), Elizabeth Dunn (X) (Seal), Wit: John Brewer, John Dunn.

Pp. 65-66: I, William Moore, Bricklayer, of Bladen County, for
₤ 10 proc. money pd. by Benjamin Clark, Planter, of
same...the moety(sic) of a tract of land jointly pattented by
me the said William Moore and him the said Benjamin Clark for
300 A, dated 1767...22 Aug 1767. William Moore (Seal), Wit:
Lawrence Byme(?), John Beard. August Court 1767. Fee paid for
recording and this Deed ordered to be Registered. Arthur Howe,
Clk. Cor.

Page 66: North Carolina, County of Bladen, James Baldwin of county
aforesaid, declare and release the son of Betty Fleater,
James Baldwin Junr to be free from all incumbrances or bondage
...1 June 1766. James Baldwin (Seal), Wit: William Dry. August
Court 1770. Prov. by Coln. William Dry, Test Maturin Colvell.

Pp. 66-67: North Carolina, County of Bladen. James Baldwin Snr,
planter, release Betty Fleater, being a true and faithful, trusty, good, obedient servant to me...1st June 1766. James
Baldwin (Seal), Wit: Willm. Dry. August Court 1770. Proven by
Wm. Dry. Maturin Colvelle.

Pp. 67-68: 22 March 1770, William McRee of Bladen County, N. C.,
planter, to Thomas Kersey of same, planter, for ₤ 25...
land on North side of Drowning Creek below Smiths bridge, whereon
John Wilson now liveth, 250 A, adj. Robert Terrill(?)...Wm McRee
(Seal), Wit: Archd. McKissak, Jacob Pope. May Court 1770. Ack.
in open Court by said McRee. Maturin Colvell, Cl.

Pp. 68-69: North Carolina, Bladen County, Richard Mallington,
for love, good will and affection to my Grandson
Richard Mallington Lewis...one Negro girl Phillis about three
years old...3 August 1768. Richd. Mallington (Seal), Wit: George
Brown, Thomas Brown. Bladen Novr Court proved by George Brown
Esqr., and ordered to be registered. A. Howe, Clk Cor.

Pp. 69-71: 6 Nov 1769, James White Esqr. Sheriff of Bladen Co.,
to William McRee Esquire of same...for recovery of
debts...a writ of benditioni exponas issuing out of the Superior
Court of Bladen 7 Feb 1769, directed sheriff to see the goods and
chattles land and Tenements of John Wilson...land on NE side Drowning Creek below Richard Smiths Bridge, adj. Robert Terrill, 250 A
for ₤ 5 s 2 d 6...James White Shff (Seal), Wit: William Smith,
Philip Wood. Prov. May Court 1770, ack. by Sheriff. Maturin
Colvell, Cl.

Pp. 71-72: Ann Pirkins of Bladen Co., planter, for ₤ 60 to John
McPhoal of Cumberland Co., N. C...land on a branch of

1738-1779

raft swamp, just below Basses last Mill Seat, 50 A granted to Ann Pirkins 25 Apr 1767...12 Dec 1768. Ana Pirkins (Seal), Wit: Solomon Johnson (∿), John Carsey(?). May Court 1769. Prov. by Solomon Johnston and ordered to be Registered. A. Howe, Clk. Cor.

Pp. 73-74: Abraham Paul of Bladen County, planter, for ₤ 30 proc. money pd. by James Stewart of same, land on S side Wilkerson swamp, adj. James Wilkerson, 100 A one half of tract of 200 A granted to William Wilkerson 24 Dec 1763, and conveyed by him to above Abraham Paul 24 June 1764, and recorded in the Register's office of said County in Book Folio 302...1 Feb 1769. Abraham Paul (Seal), Wit: James Trowell (₤), Archd. McKizsak. Prov. by Archibald McKissack, Esqr. and ordered to be registered, A. Howe, Clerk. Cor.

Pp. 74-76: 29 July 1762, Isaac Jones of Bladen Co., planter, to William Saltar of same, planter, for ₤ 100 proc. money ...land with the one half of a saw-mill in the county of Bladen on the NE side of the North West river and on a creek known by the name of Edward Jones' Creek joining a tract of land granted and patented for Joseph Singletary, and said land being granted to Thomas Russ as pr. patent 22 Nov 1738, conveyed to William Saltar decd and Isaac Jones as per deed dated 9 June 1750, 250 A being the one half of the said tract adj. Singletary...Isaac Jones (Seal), Wit: Wit: Richd. Saltar, Isaac Hill. Registered in Book E, folio 201 and recorded in the minutes of the Court.
John Burgwin.

Pp. 76-77: 6 Sept 1765, Thomas Mosely of New Hanover County and Prov. of N. C., planter, to William Saltar of Bladen Co., for ₤ 130 proc. money...land on NE side of the North West River, adj. Francis Buie, to a Black oak on the River (being Capt. George Martin's line)...granted 14 May 1735 to Edward Moseley deceased, and by his last will and testament bearing date in or about the month of March 1755 devised among other things to his son the said Thomas Moseley, the said letters Patent and will recorded in the Secretarys office of North Carolina...Thomas Moseley (Seal), Wit: A. Maclaine, John Rogers. Ack. before Robert Howe, 22 Oct 1765. Rec. Feby Court 1766. Maturin Colvill, Clrk. Bk. E. Folio 343.

Pp. 78-79: Thomas Russ of Bladen County N. C. planter, for L 50 proc. money...to William Saltar and Isaac Jones both of same, planters...tract on NE side of the North West River, on Edward Jones's Creek adj. grant to Joseph Singletary...500 A... 9 June 1750. Thomas Russ (Seal), Mary Russ (Seal), Wit: Richard singletary, Thomas Russ Junr. Ack. in open Court June 1750 by Thomas Russ. Thomas Robeson Clk C. Recotded in the Clerks office of Bladen Co., in Book C., folio No. 132, July 4th, 1750.

Pp. 80-81: North Carolina, Bladen County: Joshua Perkins of co. afsd., planter, for ₤ 150 proc. money to Richard Smith of same, planter, 125 A, half of a tract of 250 A, on a Branch of Little Pedee called Wilkersons Swamp, to the mouth of the Race path Branch, including the Plantation where the said Richard Smith lives, granted to John Odem, 17 Nov 1753, and conveyed to Benj. Davis, 20 Jan 1758, registered in the Registers office in sd. county Book E, fo. 69, and said Davis to said Joshua Perkins 1 Nov 1768, registered May Court 1769...Joshua Perkins (Seal), dated 26 April 1770. Wit: Abraham Barnes, Archd. McKissak. Prov. by Archibald McKissak May Court 1770, Maturn Colvill.

1738-1779

Pp. 81-82: James Stewart of Bladen County, Planter for ₺ 40 proc. money to Turkel McNeill of same, planter...land on N side Little Pedee on the Great Swamp commonly known by the name of Wilkerson's Swamp, 200 A granted to William Wilkerson 11 May 1753 and by deed of conveyance from sd. Wilkerson to Moses Odem and by Odem to James Wilkerson and by James Wilkerson to Abraham Paul dated 30th June 1764 and recorded in the Register's office of said County of Bladen in Book Folio 302 and by deed from said Paul to the above James Stewart dated 1 Feb 1769, proved in May Court...18 Sept 1769. James Stewart (‡) (Seal), Wit: John Odem, Arch.d McKissak. May Court 1770 prov. by Archibald Kissak, Maturin Colvill.

Pp. 83-85: James Stewart of Bladen County, planter, for ₺ 40 to Turkel McNeill...land on S side Wilkerson Swamp, adj. James Wilkersons line, 100 A, half of 200 A granted to William Wilkerson, 24 Dec 1763, conveyed to Abraham Paul 24 June 1764, then to above James Stewart 1 Feb 1767...James Stewart (‡)(Seal), Wit: John Odem, Archd. McKissak. Prov. May Court 1770 by Archd. McKissak. Deed dated 18 Sept 1769.

Pp. 85-86: North Carolina, Bladen County: James Ivey of Co. afsd. planter, for ₺ 30 proc. money to James Adair of same, Doctor...200 A in Bladen County in the fork of Little Pedee, on E side Mitchels Creek...granted to Jordan Gibson 1 July 1758, conveyed to John Wootan 25 Sept 1761, to Benjamin Davis 16 July 1762, registered in Book E, Folio 200 and by Davis to James Ivey 26 July 1766, and proved in Bladen Court by the oath of John Dunbar in Novr. 1767...15 Sept 1769. James Ivey (‡) (Seal), Wit: John McLean, Archd. McKissack. Prov. by Archibald Kissak, May court 1770. Maturin Colvill, Cl.

Pp. 87-88: 31 May 1762, Elias Fort of Edgecomb County, N. C., to John Roos of Bladen County, for ₺ 5...land on Panther branch, purchased by Fort by his Majesty by a Pattent 3 July 1756 100 A...Elias Fort (Seal), Wit: Joseph Fort, Joseph Massey (‡), Peter Rouse (~). Prov. May Court 1770, by Joseph Fort. Maturin Colvell.

Pp. 88-89: Joseph Fort of Bladen Co., N. C., planter, for ₺ 20 proc. money to Lazarus Creel of same...land on Ten Mile Swamp 100 A granted to sd. Joseph Fort 23 Oct 1761...22 April 1769. Joseph Fort (Seal), Wit: Archd. McKissak, Thomas Musselwhite. Prov. by McKissak, May Court 1770. Maturin Colville, Cl.

Pp. 89-90: Abraham Paul of Bladen Co., planter, for ₺ 30 proc. money to James Stewart...land on N side Littel Pedee on Wilkinson Swamp, 200 A granted to William Wilkinson 11 May 1753, conveyed to Moses Odem, to Jas. Wilkinson, then to Abraham Paul 31 June 1764...1 Feby 1769. Abraham Paul ( Seal), Wit: James Trowel (‡), Archd. McKissak. Prov. by Kissak, May Court 1769. A. Howe, Cor. Clerk.

Pp. 91-92: 22 July 1769, Solomon Johnson of Bladen Co., planter, to John McCrainey of same,planter, for ₺ 28 proc. money...land on Gum Swamp, east of Drowning Creek below William Driggers improvements, 100 A pattented to Solomon Johnston 22 Dec 1768...Solomon Johnston (Seal), Wit: Neil McNeil, Daniel Moody. Prov. May Court 1770, acknowledged in open court. Maturin Colvill.

10

1738-1779

Pp. 92-93: 27 Dec 1769, Richard Smith of Bladen Co., planter, to Thomas Jackson of same, planter, for Ł 4...150 A part of a survey purchased from George III, patent dated 26 Oct 1767, adj. Richard Smith...R. Smith (Seal), Wit: Aaron Odom (A), Archd. McKissak. Prov. May Court 1770, ack. by Richard Smith. Maturin Colvill, Clk.

Pp. 94-95: 28 Apr 1770, Abraham Barnes to Demsey Fiveash, planter, of Bladen Co., for Ł 20 proc. money...150 A on Eastern side of Wilkinsons upper Swamp, E. of Little Pedee, being a Pattent granted to sd. Barnes 4 May 1769...Abraham Barnes (Seal), Wit: Wm Wilkinson, Josiah Barnes. Ack. in open court, May Court 1770. Maturin Colvill, Cl.

Pp. 95-99: 13 Oct 1765, Robert Johnston Esqr. Sheriff of Bladen Co., to William Mouat of Wilmington, attorney at Law, ...by a writ of vendition exponas issuing out of the Superior Court for the Counties of New Hanover, Bladen, Conslow, Duplin and Cumberland, returnable 15 Oct inst., against the lands, etc. of Thomas Lamb of Bladen County, Store Keeper, Ł 800 s 10, at the suit of Thomas Odam...sold 200 A on 13 Aug last 1765 at the Court House in Bladen Co., for Ł 37 proc. money on Hogg Swamp about four miles from Drowning Creek...Wit: John Jones, Saml Ethridge. Ack. in open court, Nov. Court 1765. Registered in Book E, f 340. Maturin Colvill, Register.

Pp. 99-101: North Carolina, Bladen County: Joseph Cooper and wife Mary of co. afsd., for Ł 680 proc. money, to Joseph Thumbs and John Newbery Junr Wheel Wright both of same, land on Espies Creek (by the foundation of an old Grist mill formerly built by William Gray) adj. Jesse Newbery, William Gray, 167 A and another tract 640 A adj. the back land patented by McDaniel and Gray adj. James McDaniel, also 370 A, being one half of tract patented by Joseph Cooper and also one acre adj. John or Jesse Newbery's lower line...1 Nov 1768. Joseph Cooper (Seal), Mary Cooper (Seal), Wit: Edmiston Wir, Jesse Newbery. Novemr. Court 1768, ack. in open court. Arthur Howe, Clk. Court.

Pp. 101-102: North Carolina, Bladen County: Richd. Smith of co. afsd. for Ł 15 proc. money paid by Abraham Strickland of same...land on E side Drowning Creek, 100 A...1 Aug 1770. Richd. Smith (Seal), Wit: Jacob Alford, John Jones (Ɨ). August Court 1770, ack in open Court, Maturin Colville, Cl.

Pp. 102-104: 7 May 1770, Nedam Tyler of Duplin Co., N. C., to Luke Pryor of same, for Ł 100 proc. money...420 A in Bladen Co., partly a tract geanted to Moses Tyler 1757, and partly a tract conveyed from George Moore to sd. Moses Tyler and by him in his last Will and Testament bequeathed to the said Needam Tyler... by deed from George Moore 1756 for 320 A...Nedam Tyler (Seal), Wit: Rubin Ivey, Willis Grimes. Prov. Nov. Court 1770 by Rubin Tyler. Maturin Colvill, C.

Pp. 104-105: N. C., Bladen County: Philip Cheves of co. afsd., to Daniel McLean, for Ł 50 proc. money...land on E side of Wilkinsons Swamp, down the Race path Branch, the upper part of 250 A granted to John Odom 27 Nov 1753 and conveyed to James Lewis then to Benjamin Davis then to sd. Philip Cheves...21 Nov 1768. Philip Chaves (Seal), Sele Cheves (Seal), Wit: James Stewart (Ɨ), Archd. McKissak. Prov. by Archd. McKissak Esqr., May Court 1769. A. Howe, Clr. Court.

11

1738-1779

Pp. 105-107: 20 Jan 1769, John Jones & wife Christy to Henry Messar, for ℔ 45 proc. money, land in Bladen Co., 100 A on a Branch of the Litthe Marsh called the Beaver dam branch... John Jones (Seal), Charity Jones (Seal), Wit: Isaiah Powell ( ), Rosum(?) Collins. Prov. May Court (no year) by Isaiah Powell. A. Howe, Cler. Cor.

Pp. 107-108: 1 May 1770, James White of Bladen co., Esqr., to John Adear of same, weaver, for ℔ 30 proc. money...75 A on SW side of the NW branch of Cape Fear River, adj. main road, Thomas Russ's corner, John Russ...James White (Seal), Wit: John Smith, William Saltar. Prov. May Court 1770 by William Saltar. Maturin Colvell, C.

Pp. 108-109: 20 Feb 1768, Robert Greer of Cumberland County, N. C., Planter Merchant to Joseph Mercer of Bladen Co., planter, for ℔ 10...land on Drowning Creek being the Land whereon the said Mercer now lives between the mouth of Saddletree Swamp and the Raft Swamp, 150 A, a survey the said Greer purchased of our Sovereign 5 Dec 1761...Robt. Greer (Seal), Wit: Benjamin Odum(B), Thomas Moore. Prov. May Court 1770 by Benjamin Odum. Maturin Colvill, C. C.

Pp. 109-111: 7 Nov 1770, James White Esqr. of Sheriff of Bladen Co., to John Smith Esqr of same, to levy of the Chattles, etc. of Charles Hepburn and George Reynolds, decd., in the hands of Thomas Rutherford their administrator, ℔ 68 s 17 d 8½ proc. money, 320 A in Bladen Co., James White, Sheriff (Seal), Wit: Peter Lord, Jno Owen. Ack. in open Court Nov. Court 1770. Maturin Colvill, C. C:

Page 112: 23 Dec 1769, James Stewart of Bladen Co., planter, to Neill McNeil of same, planter, for ℔ 30 proc. money... land on Jobs branch 100 A, a survey of land said Stewart purchased of George II, pattent bearing date 20 Apr 1768. Wit: Nancy Fort, Solomon Johnston. August Court 1770, prov. by Nancy Fort. Maturin Colvill, C. C.

Pp. 113-114: 2 Nov 1770, Daniel Willis of Bladen Co., planter, to James Rowland Senr, Cooper, of Johnston Co., for ℔ 25 proc. money...200 A on Ashpole or Tadpole Swamp, about half a mile below the mouth of Playhill branch, pattent dated 16 Dec 1769...Danl Willis (Seal), Wit: George Willis, Thomas Rowland. Bladen County Inferior Court, Nov. 1770, ack. by Danl Willis. Maturin Colvill.

Pp. 114-115: Bladen County: William Bartram of Co. afsd., Physician, for ℔ 100 to William Bartram deceased paid by John Beard...land on Bladen County, on the NE side of the NW River, opposite to Swanns Creek now usually called Plummer Creek adj. William Mason, 250 A, granted to Moses Plummer, 9 Sept 1735, conveyed by Joseph Plummer son of said Moses Plummer to sd. William Bartram deceased, from him to me the William Bartram decd., being now the surviving son and Heir of the said decd... 7 August 1770. Wm Bartram (Seal), Wit: John Smith Junior, Ro. Edwards. Novr. 1770 Recorded in the minutes of the Court. Ordered to be registered. Test, Maturin Colvill, C. C.

Pp. 116-117: 2 August 1770, William Edwards of Prov. of South Carolina, planter, to John Clibam of Bladen Co., N. C., Laborer, for ℔ 22 proc. money...(later John Cliborn)...land

1738-1779

on Great Hogg Swamp, East of ashpole about a mile above the Lock of said Swamp, 150 A the upper part of 300 A, pattent dated 16 Dec 1769...William Edwards (X) (Seal), Wit: Danl Willis, Jesse Pitman. Bladen Court, Novr. Court 1770. Prov. by oath of John Clyburn. Maturin Colvill, C. C.

Pp. 117-118: Bladen County: Solomon Johnston Senr of co. afsd. for ₤ 20 proc. money to James Pace, 200 A, the upper part of a Tract of 600 A granted to Henry Oberry 8 Oct 1750... Solomon Johnston (2) (Seal), Wit: Richd. Smith, Daniel Moody, Prov by Richard Smith, May Court 1770. Maturin Colvill, C. C.

Pp. 118-119: 1 Aug 1770, Abraham Barnes to Isaac Lamb, planters of Bladen Co., for ₤ 30 proc. money...land on Hogg Swamp, part of a Pattent granted to Abraham Lamb, 26 Nov 1757, then deeded to Abraham Barnes 28 Apr 1764, adj. Isaac Lamb... Abraham Barnes (Seal), Wit: William Wilkinson, Shadrick Baggott. Prov. by Abraham Barnes, May Court 1770. Maturin Colvill, C. C.

Pp. 119-121: Joseph Goadon of Duplin Co., N. C., for ₤ 14 to James Odom of Bladen Co., 100 A in Bladen Co., on the old field Swamp...9 Feb 1769. Joseph Goadon (I) (Seal), Wit: Abraham Barnes, William Odom. Prov. by Abram Barnes Esqr., May Court 1770. Maturin Colvill, C. C.

Pp. 121-122: Joshua Perkins of Bladen Co., planter, for ₤ 10 proc. money to Samuel Hains of same, planter...100 A on a prong of Wilkinsons Swamp, below the mouth of Tyes Branch, granted to Joshua Perkins 22 Dec 1763...16 Sept 1769. Joshua Perkins (Seal), Wit: Aaron Adkins (A), Archd. McKissak. Ack in open court August Court 1770. Maturin Colvill, C. C.

Pp. 122-123: 24 Dec 1768, John Rutherford of New Hanover Co., N. C., Gentleman to Alexander Chapman, merchant of Bladen Co...whereas the said Alexander Chapman standeth justly indebted to sd. John Rutherford for ₤ 300 due 23 July 1770... land on NW branch of Cape Fear River, 1183 A known by the name of Brompton...Alexr. Chapman (Seal), Wit: Thos Rutherford. Wilmington, Dec. 1770. Prov. by Thomas Rutherford, M. Howard, C. J.

Pp.123-125: 8 Aug 1770, John McLuaghling of Bladen Co., N. C., Breeches maker and wife Mary, to James Bridges of same, cooper, for s 10 proc. money...land on SW side of NW River adj. to tract surveyed for John Wilkeson said to be near or on Clayton's upper line, 136 A, granted to William Singletary 28 Apr 1768... John McLaughling (X) (Seal), Mary McLaughling(↩) (Seal), Wit: Ithamar Singletary, William Hendon. Prov. Nov. Court 1770 by Ithamer Singletary. Maturin Colvill, C. C.

Pp. 126-127: Richard Smith for ₤ 40 proc. money to Moses Grice 300 A, the lower part of 640 A granted to sd. Richard Smith, 22 Dec 1768...Richd. Smith (Seal), Wit: Jeremiah Gulledge, Hardy OQuinn (X). Prov. by Richard Smith, May Court 1770. Maturin Colvill, C. C.

Pp. 127-128: N. C., Bladen Co., Daniel Norton of Bladen Co., planter to William Stewart for ₤ 100 proc. money...part of 640 A, 320 A, pattented to William Norton Senr., decd., lying on the Brown Marsh...220 A of the above 320 A left by the last will and testament of William Norton Senr, Thomas Norton and conveyed to Thomas Norton & William Norton Junr to me, and the

13

the other 100 A left to me by the will of my farther, William Norton senr...___ Sept 1770. Daniel Norton (Seal), Wit: Alexr Stewart, William McNeill. Novr. Court 1770, prov. by Wm. McNeil. Maturin Colvill, C. C.

Pp. 128-129: 23 Nov 1767, John Smith Senr of Bladen Co., planter, to Philip Ikner of same, planter, for L 17 proc. money; by patent 22 Oct 1762, 100 A on Buckhorn Swamp...John Smith (X) (Seal), Wit: Isaac Cooper, John Legett. Bladen Feby Court 1769. prov. by John Legate. A. Howe, Cler. Cour.

Pp. 129-131: 12 July 1770, James Upton, planter, of Anson Co., to Hector McNiel, planter, in Bladen co., for L 25 proc. money...land in Bladen Co., on Pugh's midle marsh swamp, granted to William Sims and conveyed to James Sims, then to William Goadson, then to John Baughart, then to sd. James Upton, 100 A...James Upton (Seal), Wit: Ro. Edward, Robt January. May, Bladen inferior Court 1771. prov. by Robert Edwards. Maturin Colvill, C. C.

Pp. 131-132: North Carolina, Bladen Co.: Anna Chase of co. afsd. to William Singletary son of Richard and Joyce Singletary of co. afsd., all my goods and chattles, household stuff and all my substance...Anna Chase (A) (Seal), Wit: Ephraim Mulford, Richd. Mullington. Prov. by both wit., Nov. Court 1764.(sic) Dated 19 Sept 1768. Registered in Book E, Folio 290. May Inferior Court 1771, Ordered to be registered. George Brown.

Pp. 132-133: 2 Aug 1770, William Edwards of Prov. of S. C., planter, to Lamb Britt, late of the County of Bladen, planter, for L 22 proc. money...land on Great Hogg Swamp, east of ashpole, 150 A, granted 16 Dec 1769...William Edwards (X) (Seal), Wit: Danl Willis, Jesse Pitman. May Bladen Court Inferior Court 1771. Prov. by Danl Willis. Maturin Colville, C. C.

Pp. 133-135: 13 Apr 1770, William Morgan of Anson Co., planter, to Goen Morgan of same, for L 20 proc. money, 100 A on NE side Drowning Creek, by Charles Oxendines improvements, granted 28 April 1768...William Morgan (WM) (Seal), Wit: James Rowland, Danl Willis. Prov. May Court 1771 by Danl Willis. Maturin Colville, C. C.

Pp. 135-136: 1 Jan 1771, Solomon Johnston Junr of Bladen Co., to Solomon Johnston St., of same, for L 50 proc. money ...200 A on S side of the East swamp, part of 600 A granted to Henry Oberry, 8 Oct 1758...Solomon Johnston (T) (Seal), Wit: Richd Smith, James Pace (X). Prov. by Richd Smith, May Court 1771. Maturin Colville.

Pp. 136-137: James Stewart of Bladen Co., planter, for L 25 proc. money to Joseph Fort of same, planter, land on Panther swamp100 A, granted to Elias Fort 26 Nov 1757, conveyed to John rouce, then to sd. James Stewart...James Stewart (I) (Seal), Wit: Archd. McKissak, John McLean. Prov. May Court 1769 by Archd. McKissak. A. Howe, Clr Cor.

Pp. 137-139: 26 Feb 1768, Joseph Fort of Bladen Co., planter, to John Hammond of same, planter, for L 10...land on N side of Saddle Tree swamp, 100 A...Joseph Fort (Seal), Wit: Henry Filby, Thomas Ivey (X). Prov. Novr. court 1768, ack. by Joseph Fort. Arthur Howe, Clr Cor.

1738-1779

Page 139: Esther Hamilton of Bladen Co., to David White of same, land on West side of NW or Cape fear River adj. upper side of Thomas Hester plantation, 200 A, for Ł 62...March ye 17th 1769. Esther Hamilton (Seal), Wit: James Ervin, Morgan Lennen. Prov. by James Ervin, Feby 26th 1771. M. Moore

Pp. 139-141: John Bound of Anson Co., N. C., planter, and wife Mary, for Ł 50 proc. money to John Cole, Cordwinder, of same....land on N side Ashpole Swamp, to the mouth of the Inden swamp, granted to David Clark 1757, conveyed to Samuel Thornton by deed, then to Stephen Cole 2 Oct 1768, 200 A...16 Jan 1769. John Bound (Seal), Mary Bound (L) (Seal), Wit: James Bound Sener, James Bound, James Hollen (O), John Terry. Prov. August Court 1770 by James Bounds Senr. Maturin Colville, C. C.

Pp. 141-142: Stephen Cole of Mecklenburg Co., N. C., for Ł 50 proc. money, to John Bounds, land in Bladen Co., on N side ashpole swamp, to the mouth of the Indian swamp, 200 A granted to David Clark, 1757...2 Sept 1768. Stephen Cole (Seal), Elener (N) (Seal), Wit: James Bound Senr., John Cole. Prov. August Court 1770 by James Bounds Senr. Maturin Colvill, C. C.

Pp. 143-144: 1 March 1767, Jesse Bound and Anne Bound of prov. of N. C., planter, to John Cole of Anson Co., for Ł 50 proc. money...land in Bladen Co., granted to Mack Cole 21 Oct 1758, on S side Drowning Creek on N side Ashpole, 300 A...Jesse Bound (Seal), Anne Bound (Seal), Wit: John Crawford, James Bound. August Court 1770. Ordered that the within deed be registered. Maturin Colvill, C. C.

Pp. 144-145: 21 Oct 1765, Mark Cole of Anson Co., to Jesse Bound of same, for Ł 50 proc. money...land on S side Drowning Creek and N side Ashpole, 160 A granted to Isaac Odom... Mark Cole (Seal), Allice Cole (Seal), Wit: Hickey Williams, John Bound. August Court 1770. Ordered that the within deed be registered. Maturin Colville, C. C.

Pp. 145-147: 8 May 1771, Barnabas Stevens of Bladen Co., planter, to Stephen Hester of same, for Ł 34 proc. money, 245 A, being half of 490 A granted to Isham Hendon 1 July 1758, adj. William McAllisters line...Barnabas Stevens (Seal), Wit: Benja. Fitzrandolph, James McDaniel. Ack. in open court May Court 1771. Maturin Colvill, C. C.

Pp. 147-148: 15 March 1771, Saml Hains of Bladen Co., to John Gibson of same, for Ł 30 proc. money, 100 A on Wilkerson Swamp, below the mouth of Tyes branch, granted to Joshua Perkins, No. 431 and dated 22 Dec 1769...Samuel Haines (Seal), Wit: Samuel Haines (Seal), Wit: Richd Smith, Jno Cade. Prov. August Court 1771, by Richd. Smith. Maturin Colell, C. C.

Pp. 148-149: Aaron Odom of Bladen Co., N. C. for Ł 55 sterling money to Mary Magee of same, spinster, land on a prong of ashpole, on the Main Road including the place where the said Odom now lives, 300 A granted to sd. Odom 10 Oct 1755...14 June 1770. Aaron Odom (A) (Seal), Wit: Thomas Odom, Nathan Britt. Prov. by Thomas Odom, August Court 1771, Maturin Colvill, C. C.

Pp. 149-151: 31 March 1746, Joseph Clark Exr. to John Worth late of Bladen Co., to Philip Wilkerson Junr of same, for Ł

1738-1779

450, 640 A on SW side of North West Branch of Cape Fear River granted to John Worth...Jos Clark (Seal), Wit: Benjamin Singletary, Esan Elliss. Proved in open court September 1746 by Esan Elliss. Thos Robeson, C. C. Recorded in the registers office of Bladen Co., Book B, folio 207, Oct. 15th, 1746. Thos Robeson, Regr.

Pp. 151-152: Charles Thompson for Ł 20 to Ignatias Flowers pltr., land on South side of Ashpole or Tadpole swamp, granted to Charles Thompson 7 Apr 1767...14 Dec 1770. Charles Thompson (Seal), Wit: Abram Baines, Wm Wilkerson. Prov. May Court 1771 by Abram Barnes. Maturin Colvill, C. C.

Pp. 152-153: 9 March 1771, Thomas Browder of Bladen Co., planter, to Christopher Sanders of same, planter, for Ł 20 proc. money, land on White Oak branch of Wagamaw Swamp, adj. Mathew Rowan Esqr., 400 A, Christopher Sanders to have 200 A... Thomas Browder (T) (Seal), Wit: Joshua Hayes, James Shipman. Prov. by Joshua Hayes, May Court 1771. Maturin Colville, C. C.

Pp. 153-155: 31 Dec 1770, Samuel Ethridge of Bladen Co., to Iver McMillan of same, for Ł 70 proc. money, land on the Brown Marsh, 200 A part of a moiety of a tract of land containing 640 A granted by Gabrial Johnston Esqr. to Mary Harnett, conveyed by sd. Mary Harnett to Solomon Lewis, and then to William Lewis, being his lawful heir, 200 A formerly sold by William Lewis to Jeremiah Bigford, adj. Jas. Campbell, Jacob Norton...the midle part of 640 A being conveyed from Patrick Stewart to Thomas Rabon by deed 17 Feb 1761, registered in Book E, folio 133, from Rabon to Samuel Etheridge which was Burnt in the office when every Record was destroyed in Maturin Colvills Term of acting as Clerk and register for the said county, and the said Samuel Etheridge and Ann his wife do hereby confirm to sd. Iver McMillan ...Saml Ethridge (Seal), Ann Ethridge (X) (Seal), Wit: Hanson Lewis, William McNiel. May Court 1771, proved by Hanson Lewis. Maturin Colville, C. C.

Pp. 155-159: North Carolina, 11 June 1763, Samuel Swann of New Hanover Co., Esqr., only Brother and heir at law of the Honorable John Swann, late of New Hanover County Esquire, decd., to Duncan McKeithan of Bladen Co., planter...whereas the said John Swann in his lifetime on or about the month of Feb. 1757 for Ł 100 proc. money to him paid by William Dry of New Hanover Co., did contract for bargain, sell and transfer unto sd. William Dry, land in Bladen Co., on N side of NW branch of the Cape fear River, about 3/4 of a mile below Walkers Bluff, 1000 A granted to John Swann 22 Sept 1728...the said William Dry on 25 Aug 1757, for Ł 150 sterling pd. by Alexander McKeithan, late of Bladen Co., did transfer to sd. Alexander McKeithan, the 1000 A...said Alex. McKeithan sold to David Lock, planter, 333 A of land, and on 29 Feb 1764, sd. David Lock for Ł 1063 s 16 d 8 proc. money did sell to Duncan McKeithan of Bladen Co., planter...remaining 667 A sold by John Swann to Duncan McKeithan...(not clear)...Samuel Swann (Seal), Wit/ Frederick Jones, Neill McNaughton, Solomon Canady, George Brown, Neill McCoulsky. Prov. in May Court 1771, by oath of George Brown. Maturin Colville, C. C.

Pp. 159-160: Abraham Paul of Bladen Co., planter, for Ł 40 proc. money to James Wilkeson of same, Laborer, 100 A on a branch of little Peedee, granted to William Moore 25 Feb 1754, to sd. Abraham Paul 24 Aug 1767 and recorded in the minutes of

1738-1779

Bladen Co. in May 1760...6 Aug 1770. Abraham Paul (Seal), Wit: Samuel Hains, Archd. McKissack. Prov. by McKissack May Court 1771. Maturin Colville, C. C.

Pp. 161-162: John Andrews of Bladen Co., for Ł 5 to son Stephen Andrews, part of a tract granted to sd. John Andrews Segner(sic) and Elizar Meredath in partnership 3 Oct 1755, 640 A this part 213 A on South River...26 Jan 1755. John Anderson (Seal) Wit: Saml Lewis, Joseph Anderson. Recorded in the minutes of said Court. Registered in the Registers office of Bladen Co. in Book E fo 35. John Burgwin, Regr.

Pp. 162-163: James Doyal of Bladen Co., planter, for Ł 20 proc. money to Edward Hailey of same...land on Ashpole Swamp, on branch of Lanes beaverdam, granted to Isaac Odom, 1 Sept 1759 & conveyance from sd. Odom to above Doyal 19 July 1765 ...20 Feb 1767. James Doyal (Seal), Wit: John Dunbar (B), Archd. McKissack. May Court 1771, prov. by McKissack. Maturin Colvill, C. C.

Pp. 163-165: 7 Nov 1768, Isaac Ceoper of Bladen Co., planter, & wife Prudence to Jesse Newbury of same, for Ł 30 proc. money...land on West side of NW river, being the place where Daniel Chancey lived, adj. Henry Sims line, opposite Chancey's house, adj. Jesse Newberry, 56 A, granted to James McDaniel, 16 Nov 1764, sold to Joseph Cooper, then to Isaac Cooper...Isaac Cooper (Seal), Prudence Cooper (P) (Seal), Wit: John Nixon, John Newbury. Prov. by John Newbury May Court 1771. Maturin Colvill, C. C.

Pp. 165-166: 10 Dec 1774, Thomas Odom of Bladen Co., to Silas Atkins of same, for Ł 20 proc. money...land on Horse Swamp, East of Ashpole or Tadpole swamp, 100 A...Thomas Odom (Seal), Wit: John Odom, Aron Odom. Prov. by John Odom, Feb. Term 1775. Alfred Moore, Clk.

Pp. 166-167: 14 Oct 1774, Henry Bird of Bladen Co., planter, to Joshua Mercer of same, planter, for Ł 35 proc. money ...the tract of land Joseph Regan took up and sold to Reubin Roberts, adj. William Pervers...Henry Bird (H) (Seal), Wit: William Moore, Nath. Richardson. Novr. Term 1774, prov. by William Moore. Alfred Moore, Clk.

Pp. 167-168: N. C., Bladen County: Stephen Hollingsworth, Cordwainer, about twenry or thirty years agone sold to Robert Edwards of same county, one half of 250 A survey on NE side of the NW River, for Ł 125 adj. John Gerves, the Registers office of this county being Burnst and the old Deed being lost the said 125 A are set over and I do hereby confirm...28 Jan 1775. Stephen Hollingsworth (Seal), Wit: James Beard, Andrew Graham. Feby Court 1775, proved by Andrew Graham. Alfred Moore, Clk.

Pp. 168-169: N. C. Bladen Co., John Stevens and his wife of the County of Cumberland, prov. afsd., to John Newbury Senr, late of Cumberland Co., part of survey on SW side of NW River between Grand and Dunns lands patented by Henry Sims for 640 A, 1755, conveyed by him to John Stevens...7 Apr 1769. John Stevens (Seal), Sarah Stevens (X) (Seal), Wit: Levi Young, Jesse Newbury. Bladen Co., Nov. 1770, prov. by Jesse Newbury. Maturin Colvill, C. C.

1738-1779

Pp. 170-171: 7 Oct 1765, Joseph Cooper of Bladen Co., planter & wife Mary, to Isaac Cooper, for Ł 20 proc. money... land on W side NW River the place where Daniel Chancey lived, adj. Henry Sims (same land as in preceding deed). Joseph Cooper (Seal), Mary Cooper (Seal), Wit: James McDaniel, Benja. Cooper. Prov. May Court 1771, by James McDaniel, Maturin Colvill, C. C.

Pp. 171-172: Robert Edwards, Surveyor of Bladen Co., for Ł 29 s 19 d 6 proc. money to Levey Ennis(?), land on NE side Drowning Creek about 8 or 9 miles above the mouth of Bear Swamp, just above an Island in the Creek...6 Nov 1771. Wit: Maturin Colvill, Evan Elliss. Prov. Novr 1771, ack. by Robert Edwards. Maturin Colvill.

Pp. 173-174: William Wilkeson of Bladen Co., indebted to Joseph Hendon Junr, for Ł 76 s 12 d 7 proc. money... mortgage 200 A on NE side of Cape Fear River, granted to Phillip Wilkeson 1735, sold to William Wilkeson 1753...17 Oct 1770. William Wilkeson (Seal), Mary Ann Wilkeson (Seal), Wit: Tho F. Robeson, Peter Robeson. May Court 1771, prov. by Thomas Robeson. Maturin Colvill, C. C.

Pp. 174-175: 19 June 1750, Phillip Wilkeson Junr of Bladen co., planter, to John Wilkeson of same, planter, for Ł 225...1/2 of 640 A belonging to John Worth decd, and conveyed to sd. Philip Wilkeson Junr by Joseph Clarke Esqr., Exr. to the said estate, land on SW side of the North west branch of Cape Fear River...Phillip Wilkeson Jur. (Seal), Wit: John Brown, Richd. Mallington. Ack. in open Court june 1750 by Wilkeson. Registers in the Registers office of Bladen co., Book C, Folio 168 July 20th 1750. Thos Robeson, Regr.

Pp. 175-177: 2 Apr 1771, Maturin Colvill of Bladen Co., to Benjamin Fitzrandolph of same, for Ł 150 proc. money... 200 A, part of a tract belonging formerly to Benjamin Fitzrandolph deceased, adj. William Singletary...Maturin Colvill (Seal), Wit: William McRee, James Bailey. Ack. in open court. Maturin Colvill, C. C., May Court 1771.

Pp. 177-178: 13 Aug 1770, Isaac Stevens and wife Sarah of Bladen Co., to William Horn of same, for Ł 80 proc. money 250 A granted by Gov. William Tryon, patent 640 A to John Wills, taking the plantation where William Sapp formerly lived...Isaac Stevens (Seal), Sarah Stevens (Seal), Wit: Chester Colsol, James Brown. Novr Court 1770, prov. by Chester Collson. Maturin Colville, C. C.

Pp. 178-180: 29 Dec 1768, Gideon Tilman of Bladen Co., to Isaac Stevens, for Ł 100 proc. money, land on S side Cabbages Swamp of Drowning Creek adj. John Wills line. Gideon Tilman (Seal), Wit: John Wills, Peregrine Johnston. Bladen Feby Court 1769, prov. by Pereygreen Johnston.

Pp. 180-181: John Conaway Senr of Dobbs co., N. C., to Ł 26 proc. money, to Josiah Taylor of Bladen Co., land in Bladen Co., on the run of Holley Branch, 266 A, part of a larger tract granted to John Conaway, including the plantation shere John Conaway Junr formerly lived...6 Feb 1769. John Conaway Senr (Seal) Wit: Joseph Oates, John Conaway. Prov. Bladen Feby Court 1769. Arthur Howe, Cler. Cor.

1738-1779

Pp. 181-182: N. C. Bladen Co.: John White and my wife Mary, planter, for L 90 to Samuel Cain, land on NE side of NW branch of Cape Fear River adj. Phillip Wilkeson...10 Apr 1758. John White (Seal), Mary White (Seal), Wit: William Elliss, Peter Robeson. Prov. by <u>Jas</u>. White, August Court (year not given) A howe.

Pp. 182-183: 10 Nov 1768, Isam Hatcher and Mary Hatcher of Bladen Co., to Isaac Stevens of same, for L 70 proc. money ...land on S side of Cabbages Swmp of Drowning Creek, 640 A granted by Gov. Tryon to John Wills, taking the plantation where William Sapp formerly lived, 250 A...Isam Hatcher (Seal), Mary Hatcher (ʃ) (Seal), Wit: Pereg. Johnston, Benjamin Buffking. Prov. by Pereygreen Johnston, Feby Court 1769. A. Howe, Cler.

Pp. 183-184: 12 June 1750, Robert Dunn of Bladen Co., planter, to Thomas Thumbs of same, for L 100...land on NW river of Cape fear a small distance below Duns Creek, part of a grant to John Dunn, conveyed to Ricahrd Dunn and by Richard Dunn to sd. Robert Dunn, 100 A...Robert Dunn (Seal), Wit: Richard Dunn, Cornelius Thims. Ack. in open court June 1750 by Robert Dunn. Registered in the Registers office Book C Folo. 134, July 4th 1750. Thos Robeson, Regr.

Pp. 184-186: John Newbury Junr, Wheelwright of Bladen Co., & wife Mary, to Joseph Thembs, for L 39 proc. money, land which was heretofore held in partnership by sd. John Newbury and Joseph Thembs, with a saw mill and grist mill and utensils, adj. William Gray and Jesse Newbury...167 A...on western side of marsh in James McDaniels back line, adj. Joseph Cooer, Neil Gray ...11 Jan 1771. John Newbury (Seal), Mary Newbury (Seal), Wit: John Beard, Jesse Thembs. August Court 1771, rpvo. by John Beard. Maturin Colvill, C. C.

Pp. 186-188: 13 Jan 1772, John Walker of Wilmington, merchant, to Thomas Henderson of Wilmington, mariner, for L 300 proc. money...640 A in two tracts on South River and Lake Creek granted to George Moore Esqr., 1 Sept 1753, and half of 640 A granted 2 Nov 1764 to Berringer Moore Esqr.; conveyed 17 Dec 1753 to Jonathan Mulky, and from Jonathan Mulky & wife Elizabeth 29 Dec 1762, conveyed to sd. Berringer Moore, and by Berringer Moore and wife Mary 14 Oct 1766, with the last mentioned tract conveyed to George Palmer, 160 A one with saw mill, conveyed by George Palmer and wife Mary Ann, to John Walker...John Walker (Seal), Wit: A McLaine. Prov. by Archibald McLaine Esqr., Feby Court 1772. Maturin Colvill, C. C.

Pp. 188-190: 27 Aug 1771, John Leget of Bladen Co., to John Mc-Cruney, of same, for L 12 proc. money...land on the mill prong of Raft Swamp about a mile above Ann Perkins survey, adj. Joseph Tuts, James Lowerys, 150 A by patent 9 Apr 1770... John Legett (Seal), Wit: Caleb Keel, Isack Wilkes. Ack. in open court, Feby Court 1772. Maturin Colvill, C. C.

Pp. 190-191: 16 July 1771, John Smith of Bladen Co., to Samuel Smith, planter, for L 70 proc. money...land, 200 A in the fork between Ashpole and Hogg swamp, granted 1 July 1758... John Smith (Seal), Wit: Danl Willis, Thomas Rowland. 1772 Feby Court, prov. by Thomas Rowland. Maturin Colvill, C. C.

1738-1779

Page 191: To the worshipful Bench of Bladen County
These may certify that I James Bailey is willing to testify on oath that he drew a Deed for a ps. of land containing 100 acres from Thomas Babon to Joseph Oates and that he saw the said Babon sign the same as his act and Deed and that he was a witness to the same and proved it in open court agreeable to law Feby 7th 1772. James Bailey. Test Maturin Colvill. Prov. Feb. Court 1772.

Pp. 191-193: 8 Aug 1771, John Oveler and wife Elizabeth, of Bladen Co., to Richard Smith of same, for ₤ 70 current money ...land on S side of the N. W. River of Cape Fear between Baker wire and Ephraum Owens land on the Main Road, 100 A, granted to Edward Davis, 10 March 1758, conveyed to sd. Oveler...John Oveler (Seal), Elizabeth Oveler (Seal), Wit: Archd. McKissack. Prov. August Court 1771, by oath of Isaac Sims, a wit. Maturin Colvill.

Pp. 193-194: 4 Aug 1770, Jacob Norton of Bladen Co., planter, to Benjamin Busby of same, for ₤ 100 proc. money...land on Brown Marsh, 200 A part of a grant of 640 A to Cornelius Harnett by Gov. Gabriel Johnston, conveyed to Solomon Lewis, then to William Lewis, to Jacob Norton...Jacob Norton (Seal), Wit: Josua Hayes, Saml Ethridge. August Court 1771, prov. by Saml Eleheridge Maturin Colvill, C. C.

Pp. 194-196: 6 March 1771, Benjamin Thomas of Bladen Co., planter, to Josiah Hendon Senr of same, for 200 barrels of Merchantable pact Tan delivered in Wilmington 10 Feb next, 200 A, the lower half of 400 A granted to Evan Thomas 20 Feb 1739 just below the mouth of a branch, Thomas Owens lower corner... Benjamin Thomas (Seal), Wit: Ithamar Singletary, William Oliver. Prov. by Ithamur Singletary May Court 1771. Maturin Colvill, C. C.

Pp. 196-197: Benjamin Singletary of Bladen Co., to son James Singletary of same, land known as the Boyd land on NE side of the North west River, 48 A, and another parcel adj. to it, 200 A...2 Feb 1771...Benjamin Singletary (Seal), Wit: Samuel Cain, Benjamin Singletary. Prov. by Benjamin Singletary, Junr., February Court 1772. Maturin Colvill, C. C.

Pp. 197-198: 15 May 1755, Maurice Moore of New Hanover Co., Gentleman, and wife Ann, to Iver McKay of Town of Wilmington, co. aforesaid, Trader, for ₤ 100 proc. money...500 A in Bladen Co., on west side of North west Branch of the cape fear River, adj. Alexander MacKay...Maurice Moore (Seal), Ann Moore (Seal), Wit: Saml Arbee, Benja. Donty. 10 Sept 1755 ack. by said Maurice and Ann his wife. Jas. Hassel(sic), C. J.

Pp. 198-200: 15 May 1755, Maurice Moore of Newhanover Co., and wife Ann, to Alexander McKay of Town of Wilmington, Trader, for ₤ 100 proc. money...land in Bladen Co., on NW branch of Cape fear, at the mouth of Hannons Creek...Wit: Saml Aslae (sic, for Ashe?), Benja. Denty. 10 Sept 1755, ack. by grantors Jas. Hassel, C. J.

Pp. 200-201: 25 July 1771, James Cameron and wife Mary, and Margaret Mackay, all of Cumberland County, N. C., planter, to Ever McKay of Bladen Co., for ₤ 120 proc. money, 150 A on west side of the Northwest branch of Cape Fear River at the mouth of Hammonds Creek, adj. Mr Pekes line...John Cameron

1738-1779

(Seal), Mary Cameron (Seal), Margaret McKay (Seal), Wit: John Cameron Junior, Sarah McFee, Jane McKay. Prov. by John Cameron Junr, August Court 1771, Maturin Colvill, C. C.

Pp. 202-203: 22 Feb 1757, John Lyon and wife Mildred of New Hanover co., to William McRee of Bladen Co., for L 135 proc. money...640 A, on SW side of the Northwest River, adj. Lees Bluff, and 144 A adj. to it, granted 9 Sept to Mathew Rowan in the 9th year of the reign of George II...John Lyon, Wit: Alexr McKuthan, Alexr McAlister. August Supreme Court at Wilmington, Ack. in open Court, Jas Hassell, Lewis Hursett(?). Registered in the registeres office of Bladen County in Book E, fo. 40. John Burgwin, Register.

Pp. 203-204: N. C., Bladen County: 25 Dec 1770, James Bailey of co. afsd., to David Morley Esqr of same, for L 20 100 A adj. the plantation of John Burgwin Esqr., known by the name of Marsh Castle...James Bailey (Seal), Wit: Neele McDuffie, James Smith. Ack. in open court by James Bailey, February Court 1772. Maturin Colvill, C. C.

Pp. 204-205: 2 Jan 1772, John Porter of New Hanover Co., N. C., gentleman, to John Smith of Bladen Co., planter, for L 400 proc. money...land in Bladen Co. on the west side of the No. W. branch of Cape Fear River aj. Iver McKay...John Porter (Seal), Wit: Hugh Monroe, Saml Smith. Recorded in the Minutes of the Court at Bladen Court House this 5th day of Feby 1772 ordered to be Registered. Maturin Colvill, C. C.

Pp. 205-206: 24 Aug 1763, William White of Bladen Co., planter, to Dinish Collom of same, for L 50 proc. money... land in Bladen Co., on N side of the No west River 320 A... William White (Seal), Wit: Mathew Byrne, Robert Edwards. Ack in open court by grantor, August Court (year not given). Registered in Book E, folio 236.

Page 207: 31 May 1771, Thomas Raburn of Orange County, to Barnabas Stevens of Bladen Co., prov. of N. C., for L 20 proc. money, 100 A in Bladen Co., on a branch of the western prong... Thomas Raburn (Seal), Wit: Alexr Stewart, Josiah Lewis. Prov. by Alexr Stewart, Augt. Court 1771. Maturin Colvill, C. C.

Page 208: 31 March 1771, Solomon Mercer Senr of prov. of N. C., planter, to Noah (Noar) Mercer of Bladen Co., planter, for L 5 proc. money...78½A as is patented for Solomon Mercer 26 Oct 1767...Solomon Mercer (Seal), Wit: Joseph Mercer, Maluchi Mercer. Prov. by Joseph Messer, Novr Court 1771. Maturin Colvill, C. C.

Pp. 208-210: N. C., Bladen Co.: Stephen Hollingsworth, Cordswainer, for L 150 proc. money to Samuel Hollingsworth of Cumberland County and prov. afsd., tract on NE of the NW of Cape Fear River, 150 A patent 13 Sept 1735, Rec. 19 Jan 1735/6 to Richard Dunn, conveyed 13 Dec 1737; also 150 A patented by John Linscom 9 Sept 1735, conveyed 8 May 1741...29 Apr 1770. Stephen Hollingsworth (Seal), Wit: John Hollingsworth, Ro. Edwards. Prov. in open court by Robert Edwards, May Inferior Court 1772. Maturin Colvill, C. C.

Page 210: 31 March 1770, Solomon Mercer Senr of prov. of N. C., planter, to Nour Mercer of Bladen Co., for L 2 s 10 proc.

21

1738-1779

money...25 A on Thick Branch...Solomon Mercer (Seal), Wit: Joseph Mercer, Malachi Mercer. Prov. by Joseph Mercer, Novr Court 1771 Maturin Colvill, C. C.

Pp. 211-213: 6 May 1772, James White Esqr late Sheriff of Bladen Co., to John Burgwin...by a writ of fieri facias issued out of Superior Court held at Wilmington 26 May on the goods and chattels of Bunbury Day decd in the Hands of Bridgell Beaty administratrix to be levied ⟶ 200 proc. money, at the suit of John Burgwin and Hugh Waddle...land on Black River in Bladen Co., patented to George Moore Esqr 1 Sept 1753 and 2 Nov 176 and in two several Indentures from George Palmer and Mary Ann his wife to John Walker and the said Bunbury Day, 20 June 1768 and 16 May 1769, 320 A and 100 A on west side Black River adj. John Howard Neel Straken... patent to Bunbury Day 5 May 1769, and 90 A by indenture of conveyance 20 Apr 1768, between Sarah Straken and said Bunbury Day...1410 A and saw Mill...now for ⟶ 300 s 4 proc. money...James White (Seal), Wit: A Maluine. Ack. in open court by James White, May Court 1772.

Pp. 213-214: 15 Jan 1771, Luke Prior of Duplin Co., N. C., planter, to Mathew Pridgen of same, planter, for ⟶ 70 proc. money...land in Bladen Co., on west side of South River adj. George Moore, granted to said George Moore 1751, conveyed to Mosses Tyler, and by the said Moses Tyler in his last will to Needham Tyler and by Needham Tyler to said Luke Prior by deed; also 100 A on west side Black River between the tract before granted and Othiel Strahams former place, both tracts 420 A, the last 100 A granted to Moses Tyler 1757, and by Moses Tyler in his last will to his son Needham Tiler...Luke Prior (Seal), Wit: John Yarbrough, James Yarbrough, William Pridgen. Prov. by William Pridgeon Nov. Court 1771, Maturn Colvill, C. C.

Pp. 214-216: 1 Jan 1771, John King and wife Jane of Bladen Co., to Peter Byrne of same, for ⟶ 60 proc. money...103 A on NE side of NW River adj. John Torster, being part of a tract sold by said John Torster to James Moorehead and John King marrying the Daughter of James Moorehead, the said 103 A became his patent 1760...John King (Seal), Jane King (Seal), Wit: William Moorehead, James Moorehead. Ack. in open court Nov. Court 1771. Maturin Colvill, C. C.

Pp. 216-217: 7 Jan 1772, James Lowery of Bladen Co., planter, to Daniel Smith of same, planter, for ⟶ 15 proc. money land on Bladen Co., below Joshua Brawlevys(?) land the place where Daniel Smith now lives, granted to James Lowery 26 Oct 1767... James Lowery (Seal), Wit: John McCainey, Hugh Brown, Daniel McLaughlan. Prov. by Hugh Brown, May Court 1772. Maturin Colvill, C. C.

Pp. 217-218: N. C. Bladen Co.: James Lowery, planter, for ⟶ 20 proc. money to John Zuilley, planter, (Later appears to be John Fairley), land on Drowning Creek about 2 Miles above the head of the White Oak Swamp, granted 18 May 1771, 200 A... dated _____ 1772. James Lowery (Seal), Wit: Hugh Brown, John Gilchrist, Joseph Fort. Prov. by Joseph Fort, May Term 1772. Maturin Colvill, C. C.

Pp. 218-219: N. C. Bladen Co., Joseph Fort for ⟶ 32 proc. money, to John Gilchrist planter, land on Mill prong of

22

1738-1779

Raft swamp, part of a survey to me granted Dec 1770, adj. Obenys (sic, for Oberrys?) patent, John McCaineys, 150 A...23 Apr 1772. Joseph Fort (Seal), Wit: Hugh Brown, John McCrainey. Ack. in open court May term 1772. Maturin Collvill, C. C.

Pp. 219-220: N. C. Bladen County: Joseph Fort planter for Ł 32 proc. money, to John McCainey, planter...land on mill prong of Raft Swmp, 195 A granted Dec 1770, adj. Henry Obenys, John Gilchrist... Apr 1772. Joseph Fort (Seal), Wit: Hugh Brown, John Gilchrist. Ack. in open court May term 1772. Maturin Colvill, C. C.

Pp. 221-222: 27 Dec 1771, John Bryan & wife Jane of Bladen Co., to John McRown of same, for Ł 15 proc. money...land on Brown Marsh, 100 A, a moiety of 200 A granted to sd. John Bryan, by Arthur Dobbs, 26 Nov 1757, adj. Nickland branch...Jane Bryan (Seal), John Bryan (Seal), Wit: Wm Smith, Benja. Singletary. Ack. in open Court May Court 1772. Maturin Colvill, C. C.

Pp. 222-223: James White, late Sheriff of Bladen Co., at inferior Court of Pleas and Quarter Sessions held for Bladen Co.. 7 Feb 1771, a Judgment was recovered by Thomas Rabon against ilvanus Wilson, administrator of the goods and Chattles, etc. of John Small deceased, for Ł 13 s 7 proc. money...130 Aon NE side of the North west River adj. John Linscombes land, sold to highest bidder 7 May 1771..15 Feb 1772. James White (Seal), Wit: James Richardson, John Legett. Ack. in open Court, May Court 1772. Maturin Colvill, C. C.

Pp. 224-225: 6 Dec 1766, Benjamin Cooper of Bladen Co., Yeoman, to Silvanus Wilson of Cumberland Co., planter, for Ł 60 proc. money...land on NE side of the Northwest River on the upper fork of Hollingsworths Creek, back of Hollingsworth land, granted 25 Sept 1754 to sd. Benjamin Cooper, 300 A...Benja. Cooper (Seal), Wit: Joseph Cooper, Emiston Weir, John Legett. Prov. by John Legget, "Bladen Court 1772." Maturin Colvill, C. C.

Pp. 225-226: 6 Dec 1767, Benja. Cooper, Joseph Cooper and Mary Cooper of Bladen Co., Yeoman, to Silvanus Wilson of Cumberland Co., planter, Joseph Cooper and Mary his wife and Benjamin Cooper...150 A on NE side North west River on the upper fork of Hollingsworth Creek adj. Benja Coopers Jumper Swamp, patent 18 Nov 1760...Benja. Cooper (Seal), Joseph Cooper (Seal), Mary Cooper (Seal), Wit: John Legett, Edmiston Weir. Prov. May Court 1772, by John Legett. Maturin Colvill, C. C.

Pp. 227-228: 3 Feb 1770, John Johnston of Cumberland Co., planter, to Silvanus Wilson, planter, for Ł 25 proc. money... land in the said County of Cumberland on the East side of the Northwest River it being the place where Titus Overton lived, 100 A, granted to Thomas Fenney 15 Nov 1755, and made over said tract to John Johnston...John Johnston (Seal), Wit: John Elwell, Benja. Elwell, K. Sharp. Prov. August Court 1771, by Benjamin Elwell. Maturin Colvill, C. c.

Pp. 228-229: 21 Oct 1755, Mark Cole of Anson Co., to Jesse Bounds of same, for Ł 50 proc. money...land on County of Blaton (sic), 300 A on the South side of Drowning Creek on N side Ashpole...Mark Cole (Seal), Alice Cole (Seal), Wit: Herkey Williams, John Bound. August Court 1770. Ordered that the within deed be Registered. Maturin Colvill, C. C.

23

1738-1779

Pp. 229-231: 29 June 1768, George Palmer of Bladen Co., planter, and wife Mary Ann to John Walker of Wilmington, merchant, for ₤ 230 proc. money...land on South River & Lake Creek also 320 A adj. to it, tracts granted to George Moore, 1 Sept 1753, and sd. George Moore by two deeds 17 Dec in the year last aforesaid conveyed to Jonathan Malky and by said Jonathan Malky and wife Elizabeth by Deed 29 Dec 1762, conveyed to Benjamin Moore, and also one half of all that other tract of 640 A on Lake Creek and South River adj. Barringer Moores land, granted 2 Nov 1764 to Berringer Moore, and by sd. Berringer Moore and wife Mary, with the above mentioned two tracts by indenture 13 Oct 1766 conveyed to sd. George Palmer, with half of a saw mill and improvements. George Palmer (Seal), Mary Ann Palmer (Seal), Wit: A. Maclaine, W. Gregory. Prov. May Court by Archibald McLane, Esqr. Maturin Colvill, C. C.
[In the above deed appears a blank space and the following notation: "This Blank shows that the old Book obliterated so it could not be read."]

Pp. 232-233: N. C. Bladen County: James White, late Sheriff of said co., whereas at a Superior Court held for the District of Wilmington upon 27 Nov 1770, a Judgment was recovered by Thomas Griffeth of the Kingdom of Great Britain against Aaron Odon, for ₤ 53 s 14 proc. money...later Aaron Odom, 200 A on both sides of the Main Road leading from John Ovelers over Drowning Creek, sold 7 May 1771...dated 15 March 1772. James White Coroner (Seal), Wit: Maturin Colvill, William Saltar. Prov. May Court 1772, ack. by James White. Maturin Colvill, C. C.

Pp. 234-236: 4 Feb 1772, James White Esqr late Sheriff of Bladen Co., to William Saltar of same, planter, by writ of fiere facias from Superior Court held at Wilmington, 27 Nov 1771 to levy of the lands and Tenements of Elizabeth Donaldson decd in the hands of Thomas Rutherford, administrator, land on SW side of the Northwest branch of Cape Fear River adj. the lower side of William Hawksworths land, 640 A...James White (Seal), Wit: Isaac Jones, Benja. Humphrey. N. C. Bladen Co., Febry Court 1772, Ack. in open court. Maturin Colvill, C. C.

Pp. 236-237: James White, late Sheriff of Bladen Co., at an Inferior Court held for Bladen Co., first Tues. in August 1768, recovered by Elias Burgeson against James Baggot for ₤ 2 s 8 proc. money...300 A on Saddel Tree Swamp on the NE side of Drowning Creek...26 March 1772. James White (Seal), Wit: James Council, William Saltar. Ack. in open Court, May Court 1772. Maturin Colvill, C. C.

Pp. 237-239: 1 May 1769, David Russ admr. Bridget Chambers admr. of William Chambers decd. Bladen Co., to James White of same, that David Russ & Bridget Chambers, for ₤ 21 proc. money ...land on SW side of NW branch of Cape Fear River 75 A on the main road, adj. Thomas Russes corner...David Russ (Seal), Bridget Chambers (Seal), wit: Wm McRee, George Brown. Prov. by George Brown, August Court 1770. Maturin Colvill, C. C.

Pp. 239-240: 6 Aug 1772, Maturin Covill Exr. of the last will and testament of Owen Brady late of Bladen Co., planter decd., to Thomas Owen of same, Esquire, whereas the said Owen Brady by his last will and testament bearing date on or about 17 May in the year aforesaid did appoint Maturin Colvill to make a deed for 200 A on SW side of the NW branch of Cape Fear River adj.

24

1738-1779

Josiah Hendon Senr, as soon as the said Thomas Owen should pay
Ł 250 to the sd. Maturin Colvill...200 A on SW side of the NW
river adj. upper side of land formerly the property of William
Cain, granted by George II 20 Feb 1735 to David Lewis...Maturin
Colvill (Seal), Wit: A. McLaine, Henry Gifferd. Ack. in open
Court, August term 1772.

Pp. 240-242: 26 Dec 1770, Roger Barefield, planter, of Bladen
Co., & William Barefield, planter,of Dobbs Co.,, the sd.
Roger Barefield & Precilah his wife, for Ł 30 proc. money, pd.
by said William Reynolds, 300 A on Flowers Swamp west of Drowning
Creek, the lower part of 500 A on Western Hill side of said Swamp
near his own lower line, patent granted to James Blunt 4 May 1769
conveyed to Roger Barefield by deed 13 Apr 1770...Roger Bearfield
(Seal), Wit: Edward Flowers, James Inman. August Court 1771, prov.
by Edward Flowers. Maturin Colvill, C. C.

Pp. 242-243: Joshua Hays of Bladen Co., Sadler, for Ł 16 s 10
proc. money, pd. by Luther Hays, planter...150 A,
a plantation formerly belonging to James Clark Senr on East side
of     branch, Dunns branch...26 Aug 1760. Joshua Hayes (Seal),
Wit: John Dunn (†H), Samuel Thornton. Prov. August Court 1760,
ack. by Joshua Hays, John Burgwin. Registered in Book E, Fol.
112. J. Burgwin, Regr.

Page 244: Caleb Cowpland, of Town & County of Chester in the Prov.
of Pennsylvania, have appoint trusty friend Isaac Jones
of County of Bladen, N. C., lawful attorney, to sue for and Reco-
ver from any person, land on NW branch of Cape Fear River, and
to sell3 Aug 1753. Caleb Cowpland (Seal), Wit: Jonath Evans, Cornelius Thembs, Henry hale Graham. Prov. in open Court by Jonathan
Evans Esqr. Thos Robeson, Clk. Registered in Bladen Co., Book D
Folio No. 129. December 27th 1753. Thos Robeson, Regr.

Page 245: 17 Apr 1741, Peter White of Bladen Co., Millwright, for
Ł 200 to Edward Jones, 400 A and ½ part of saw Mill
built upon said land, part of the tract whereon Edward Jones now
liveth on Northwest River...Peter White (Seal), Wit: David L Loyd,
Mary Lock (⌒). Registered June 20th 1741 Pr John Clayton Regr.

Pp. 246-247: John Protherow(?) of Bladen Co., planter, for Ł 300
to Isaac Jones, land adj. upper side of Edward Jones
250 A...patent to sd. Priothrow 5 Sept 1735...18 June 1748. John
Perddro (Seal), Margaret Prothrou (Seal), Wit: Thomas Jones, Sam
Richardson.   Thomas Jones proved in open court June 1748. Thos.
Robeson Clk. Registered in Book B, folio 397, July 13th 1748.

Pp. 247-248: 5 March 1741, David Lloyd of Bladen Co., Blacksmith,
for Ł 50 NC currency to Isaac Jones, 400 A and ½ part
of a saw mill, part of land whereon Edward Jones now liveth on
NW River adj. John Protherough...David Lloyd (Seal), Wit: Alexr
Edwards, Jno Bowdey. Registered June 20th 1741 Pr. John Clayton,
Register.

Pp. 248-249: Richard Singletary Senr of Bladen Co., Yeoman, by
grant executed by the Lords proprietors 22nd Oct
1728, 1000 A on S side of the No wt branch of Cape Fear River about
4 miles below the Copper mines, 350 A of said tract with a negroe
man named Prince, by deed of gift bearing date 20 Dec 1744, Registered in Bladen Co., Dec. 28th 1744 in Book B, folio No 10, that
I the said Richard Singletary for the love good will and affection

1738-1779

to my son in law Isaac Jones...land adj. to Thomas Ornies upper line...15 Dec 1747. Richard Singletary (Seal), Wit: Sampson Wood, Thos Robeson. Prov. Dec. 1747 court by Thomas Robeson. Registered in Book B, folo No. 350. Dec. 26 1747. Thomas Robeson, Regr.

Pp. 249-250: 9 May 1767, William White, Merchant of Bladen Co., to Isaac Jones of co. aforesaid, planter, for L 106 proc. money...land on NW branch of Cape Fear River, S side, adj. land formerly called Griffeth Jones land, adj. William Chambers...William White (Seal), Wit: William Encek, Ganel White. Prov. Feby Court 1769, by ack. Wm White. Arthur Howe, Cler Cor.

Page 251: 5 March 1741, David Lloyd of Bladen Co., Blacksmith, for L 110 NC currency to Edward Jones of Bladen Co., carpenter, 400 A and 1/8 part of a saw mill, part of tract where Edward Jones now liveth...David Lloyd (Seal), Wit: Alexr Edwards, John Bowdey. Registered June the 20th 1741, Pr. John Clayton, Regr.

Pp. 251-253: 1 May 1746, Samuel Baker Esqr of Bladen Co., to John Brown, of same, carpenter, for L 400...land on SW side of NW branch of Cape Fear River adj. Griffeth Jones, William Bartrum, 448 A...Saml Baker (Seal), Wit: John Budbedg, John Dowlass. Ack. in open Court Sept 1746 by Saml Baker Esqr. Registered in Book B, Folo No. 168, September the 23rd 1746. Thos Robeson, Register.

Pp. 253-254: 27 Feb 1765, Ann Nessfield Executrix & John Robeson Executor of L. W. & T. of John Nessfield late of Bladen Co., Farmer, decd., to William White Merchant & Isaac Jones planter...whereas the said John Nessfield by his L. W. & T. bearing date 27 March 1764 willed that all his lands should be sold ...for L 200 proc. money, land on SW side of the NW branch of Cape Fear River adj. land formerly called Griffith Jones, land formerly belonging to William Chambers, 448 A...Ann Nessfield (Seal), John Robeson (Seal), Wit: Saml McRee, Jno Grange Junr. May Court 1776, prov. by Saml McRee. Registered in Book E, folio 318. Maturin Colvill, Regr.

Pp. 255-256: 4 Aug 1754, John Brown of Cumberland Co., N. C., Millright to John Jessfield of Bladen Co., for L 70 proc. money..land on SW side of NW River adj. Griffeth Jones, William Chambers...John Brown (Seal), Mary Brown (Seal), Wit: William Cain, Danl Willis. Ack. in open court Nov. 1754 by John Brown Esqr. Mary Brown privately examined surrendered her Dower. Registered in Book D, fol. No. 195, Nov. 22, 1754. Thos Robeson, Regr.

Page 256: Edward Davis of Bladen Co., Bricklayer, for L 80 proc. money...to Isaac Jones, negro woman Phillis aged about 28 years...31 July 1754. Edward Davis (Seal), Wit: John McWhorter, Jno Lennon. Prov. by John Lennon August 1754, Thos Robeson. Recorded in Book D, folo. 173, Augt 26th, 1754.

Page 257: Samuel Baker of Bladen precinct, Blacksmith, for L 20 proc. money to Edward Jones & David Loyd of same...1/3 part of a tract of land and ¼ part of a share of the Mill erected upon said land, whereon the said Edward Jones now liveth. 18 Aug 1737. Saml Baker (Seal), Wit: William Holt, Reuben Waid. (No rec. date given and no prov. date.)

26

1738-1779

Pp. 257-258: William Larkins of New Hanover Co., N. C., for ₤ 5 to Edward Jones of Bladen Co., half tract of land 320 A, part of a tract of 640 A granted to John Larkins adj. Roger Haynes, the upper half being conveyed over to Edmund Rowke ...2 Oct 1746. William Larkins (Seal), Wit: Richd Mullington, Elisha Maxwell. Prov. by Richard Mallington, Dec. 1746. Rec. in Book B, folo. No. 234, Decr ye 31/1746. Thos Robeson, Clk.

Pp. 258-259: 24 Feb 1763, William Singletary, planter of Bladen Co., to Benjamin Carpenter of same, for ₤ 25 proc. money...(later refers to grantee as Benjamin Moore)...500 A on East side of NW River, on Edward Jones Creek, adj. Thos Russes corner. William Singletary (Seal), Wit: John Nessfield, Robert Wise. Feby Inferior Court 1763, ack. in open court. Recorded in Book E, Folio 206. J. Burgwin, Regr.

Page 260: 29 Feb 1764, Benjamin Moore, Carpenter, of Bladen Co., to William Saltar, for ₤ 25 proc. money...500 A on Edward Jones Creek, adj. Thos Russ. BenjaminMoore (Seal), Wit: David Russ, William Singletary. Bladen Co., Feby Court 1764, ack. in open Court. Maturin Colvill, C. C.

Page 261: Joseph Howard of Bladen Co., for good will and affection, to son Benjamin Howard of same, 150 A on Rouns branch, adj. Hezekiah Howards Dwelling House, John Howards head line...15 Apr 1772. Joseph Howard (Seal), Wit: John Howard, William Lewis, Othniel Straken. Prov. by John Howard, May Court 1772. Maturin Colvill, C. C.

Pp. 261-263: 17 Apr 1771, Benjamin Stone of Brunswic County, N. C., to Maturin Colvill of Bladen Co., for ₤ 300 proc. money...640 A on NE side of the Northwest Branch of Cape Fear River, adj. lands formerly belonging to James Boone, lands formerly belonging to Edward Randolph Junr, and by the river... Benjamin Stone (Seal), Wit: Thos Henderson, David Ross. April 19, 1771, Recd. sum of ₤ 300 pounds proc. . Benja. Stone. Prov. by David Ross, 7 Dec 1771. Richard Henderson.

Pp. 263-264: 25 Apr 1771, James Blount of Prov. of South Carolina, planter, to John Flowers, of Edgecomb, N. C., planter, for ₤ 64 proc. money...land on W side lrowning Creek being the place where James Roberts formerly lived, 200 A, the lower part of 300 A patented by Thomas Ivey, 29 Sept 1756, conveyed to said James Blount & the deed left in the office which deed is said to be Burnt...James Blount (Seal), Wit: Jesse Pitman, Edward Flowers. August Court 1771, prov. by Edward Flowers. Maturin Colvill, C. C.

Pp. 264-266: 23 May 1772, Joseph Britton & Stephen Britton of Bladen Co., planters, to Josiah Wilson of same, planter, for ₤ 100 proc. money, 300 A on NE side of the NW River between lands of George Martin & Doctor Thomas Hall, granted to John David 1736, conveyed by Davis to William White 18 March 1737, by said White to William Bartram 8 Nov 1743, then to Anthony Golly 19 March 1750, to Edmund Logatie 18 Feb 1768, by an assignment on the back of the last mentioned deed dated 7 July 1768, conveyed to Joseph Britton and Stephen...Joseph Britton (Seal), Stephen Britton (Seal), Wit: Joseph Lock, Daniel Melvin. August Court 1772, prov. by Joseph Lock. Maturin Colvill, C. C.

1738-1779

Pp. 266-268: 5 Nov 1771, James White, Esqr late Sheriff of Bladen Co., to William Saltar of same, planter...by writ of fiere facias from court at Wilmington 27 Nov 1771, to levy ₺ 42 s 8 d 9 from goods and chattels of John Dolzall decd., in the hands of Thomas Rutherford his administrator...land on NE side of NW River adj. Moses Plumbers land, 430 A. James White sheriff (Seal), Wit: David Lindsay White, Alexr Harvey. Ack. in open court, Nov. Court 1771, Maturin Colvill, C. C.

Pp. 268-269: 3 May 1768, John White of Bladen Co., to his two sons James White & Griffeth White both of co. afsd., for ₺ 45 proc. money...land on NE side of NW branch of Cape Fear River, 200 A...John White (Seal), Wit: Ithamar Singletary, William Saltar. Bladen Court, May 1772. Maturin Colvill, C. C. Prov. by William Saltar.

Page 270: 14 May 1771, Thomas Simpson of Bladen Co., to Benjamin Thomas, of same, planter, for ₺ 60 proc. money...land on Bakers Creek adj. John Graedys line...Thomas Simson (Seal), Wit: John Oveler, Philemon Bryan. Prov. by John Oveler, May Court 1772. Maturin Colvill, C. C.

Page 271: 7 May 1772, Benja. Thomas of Bladen Co., to Richard Smith of same, for ₺ 40 proc. money...land on Bakers Creek otherwise Greens Creek...Benjamin Thomas (Seal), Wit: James Johnston, Maturin Colvill. Prov. by Maturin Colvill, May Court 1772.

Pp. 272-273: 25 Apr 1771, Martha Blount, Widow of prov. of South Carolina, to John Flowers of Edgecomb Co., N. C., planter, for ₺ 36 proc. money...land on W side Drowning Creek, part of the land where James Roberts formerly lived 100 A, the upper part of 300 A, Thomas Ivey patentee, 29 Sept 1756, conveyed to James Blount of Bladen Co., which deed was left in the Clerks office & is said to be burnt & then conveyed to the said James Blount by a deed to Martha     of Bladen County which is the aforesaid Martha Blount now of South Carolina, the deed bearing date 3 Feb 1769. Martha Blunt (Seal), Wit: Jesse Pitman, Edwd Flowers. Augt Court 1771, prov. by Edward Flowers. Maturin Colvill, C. C.

Page 273: Edward Jones of Bladen precinct, N. C., Carpenter, for ₺ 5 NC currency, to Hannah Jones of same, half of tract known as Jones Burrough...13 Oct 1738. Edwd Jones (Seal), Wit: Gabriel Wayne, Wm Saltar. Mar Court 1738/9, ack. in open court. Registered July 15, 1739. Richd Hellur, Regr.

Pp. 274-275: 9 Sept 1771, John Lock & wife Elizabeth of Bladen Co., to Thomas Lock son of said John Lock, planter, for ₺ 5 proc. money...part of tract known as Jones Burrough, granted to Edward Jones 5 Sept 1735, for 640 A, about a mile above the place called the Cooper mines...John Lock (seal), Elizabeth Lock (Seal), Wit: John Beard, Isaac Ray. Bladen Court, May 1772, prov. by Isaac Ray. Maturin Colvill, C. C.

Pp. 275-276: 29 Mar 1772, Nathan Horn of Bladen co., to John Flowers of Edgecomb Co., for ₺ 30 proc. money...land in Bladen Co., on Flowers & Cowards swamps SW of Drowning Creek near Coles Bluff, adj. Hector McNeills line, patent dated 22 Dec 1770. Nathan Horn (Seal), Wit: Danl Willis, Jesse Pitman. May Court

1738-1779
1772, by Daniel Willis, Maturin Colvill, C. C.

Pp. 277-278: 3 Aug 1772, Joseph Fort to Neil McNeill of Bladen
Co., for Ł 10 proc. money...land on Jobs branch west
of the NOrth prong of the Raft Swamp, adj. James Stewart, William
Carver, 100 A...Joseph Fort (Seal), Wit: Wm McRee, thos Robeson
Junr. Ack. in open Court Aug. 1772. Maturin Colvill, C. C.

Pp. 278-279: 3 Apr 1770, Richard Thomas of Bladen Co., to Thomas
Owen of same, Millwright, for Ł 40 proc. money...
200 A, ½ of 400 A granted to Evan Thomas 20 Feb 1739...Richard
Thomas (Seal), Wit: Ithamar Singletary, Benjamin Thomas. Prov.
May Court 1770; Maturin Colvill, C. C. Ack. in open Court.

Pp. 279-280: Ephraim Manning of Midlesex Co., Prov. of East
Jersey, Carpenter, have appointed his brother in law
Benjamin Fitzrandolph of Cape Fear, planter, his lawful attorney
to dispose of tracts in North Carolina or Cape Fear. 15 Nov 1739.
Ephraim Manning (Seal), Wit: John Lockwood, John Knox, Jno
Harnicks.

Pp. 280-281: Benjamin Fitzrandolph of Bladen Co., my authority of
power of attorney granted me by my Brother in law
Ephraim Manning of Middlesex Co., East New Jersey, for Ł 300 NC
money to John Owen of Bladen Co., planter, land on N Side of NW
branch of Cape Fear River, 640 A, whereon the said John Owen now
dwelleth... 18 June 1740. Benjan. Fitzrandolph (Seal), Wit: Wm
Bartram, Stephn. Brock. Prov. in open court by Benjamin Fitzrandolph, June Court 1740. Richd. Hellur, C. C. Ro. Edwards, Regr.

Pp. 281-282: 15 Apr 1772, Duncan McKeithan of Bladen Co., to Peter
Broades of same, planter, for Ł 85, 137 A on NE side
NW River, adj. Allen McDugald, about 3/4 mile below Walkers Bluff
...15 Apr 1772. Duncan McKeithan (Seal), Isabel McKeithan (Seal)
Wit: Wm McRee, Stephen White, Donald McKeithan, John Brown. May
Court 1772, ack. in open court, Maturin Colvill, C. C.

Pp. 283-284: 1 May 1772, Richard Smith of Bladen Co., planter, to
Neill McFall of same, for Ł 94 proc. money...land on
E side Drowning Creek, 200 A about a mile above Over Sheets Bridge
by deed of conveyance William Pace to sd. Richard Smith, Rec. in
Cumberland County, Augt Court 1763, Registered in said County in
Book B, folo 168, the other tract 340 A near Smiths old corner,
upper part of 640 A granted to Richard Smith 2 Dec 1768...Richard
Smith (Seal), Wit: Daniel McLaughlan, Thomas Bird. May Court
1772, ack. in open court. Maturin Colvill, C. C.

Pp. 284-285: Joseph Oates of Bladen Co., for Ł 20 proc. money to
Carraway Oates of same, planter, land on Swamp called
Ashpole or Tadpole, 100 A, granted to Richard Barfield to James
Cole, then to Thomas Robeson then the said Thomas Robeson by power
of attorney to Joseph Oates, 6 Feb 1772. Joseph Oates (Seal), Wit:
Smith, William Grantham. Feby Court 1772, ack. in open court.
Maturin Colvill, C. C.

Pp. 285-286: 25 Apr 1771, James Blount of prov. of South Carolina,
planter, to John Flowers of Edgecomb Co., N. C.,
for Ł 30 proc. money...land on Flowers Swamp west of Drowning
Creek, 200 A, the upper part of 500 A granted 4 May 1769...James
Blount (Seal), Wit: John Pitman, Edward Flowers. August Court
1771, prov. by Edward Flowers. Maturin Colvill, C. C.

1738-1779

Pp. 286-287: 4 Apr 1772, Farquard Campbell of Cumberland Co., N. C., Gentn., to Adam Ivey, planter, of Bladen Co., for Ł 30 proc. money, 200 A on Hogg Swamp, patent 6 May 1760... Farquhard Campbell (Seal), Wit: John McKay, Danl Willis. May Court 1772, prov. by Daniel Willis, Maturin Colvill, C. C.

Pp. 288-289: 6 Aug 1771, George Ikner of Bladen Co., planter, to Phillip Ikner of same, for Ł 40 proc. money...land on N side Pughs Little Marsh, 100 A, granted to John Johnson Jr., 15 Nov 1753, being the place where Oxendine formerly lived, by deed 1 Oct 1757, conveyed to Thomas Field of Johnson Co., conveyed to Sumerset Donehow by deed 20 July 1763, then to George Ikner by deed 1 Sept 1763...George Ikner (Seal), Wit: Wm Maulsby, Willm. Barlow. Prov. May Court 1772, ack. in open court. Maturin Colvill, C. C.

Pp. 289-290: 18 Feb 1768, Anthony Golley of Philadelphia, Mariner, to Edmond Logartie of Bladen Co., N. C., planter, for Ł 150 proc. money...land on NE side of Cape Fear River between lands of George Martin, Doctor Thomas Hall, granted to Jno Davis 1736, conveyed to William White, 18 March 1737, to William Bartram 8 Nov 1743, sold to Anthony Golley 19 March 1750...Anthony Golley (Seal), Wit: David Smith, Isa Parvisol.

Page 290: In consideration of Ł 150 proc. money paid by Joseph Britton & Stephen Britton of Bladen Co., planters, I sell the above mentioned parcel of land. 7 July 1768. Edmond Logartie (Seal), Wit: Marmadrake Jones. Prov. by David Smith, 31 May 1772. M. Moore. Prov. by Marmadrake Jones, 30 May 1772, Richard Henderson.

Pp. 290-292: 5 Oct 1769, Alexander Chapman of Bladen Co., Merchant, to Thomas Owen, Millwright, for Ł 40 proc. money, land on SW side of the Northwest River 1040 A; the first tract 640 A, adj. Evan Thomas upper corner, James Lyon, granted to Alexander Chapman, 28 Apr 1768,the other tract 400 A...Alexander Chapman (Seal), Wit: Richd Saltar, Jno Owen. Ack. in open court, May Court 1770. Maturin Colvill, C. C.

Pp. 292-293: N. C., Bladen County: Stephen Hollingsworth, miller, & wife Mary of co. afsd., for Ł 450 to Samuel Hollingsworth, 640 A on NE side of the Northwest River adj. Alexander Grant, Saml Johnston, excepting the privilege of a Saw Mill already granted to William Lord...7 Oct 1744. Stephen Hollingsworth (Seal), Wit: John Dunn, Volentine Hollingsworth. March Court 1745, Prov. by Valentine Hollingsworth. Registered April 2, 1745, Bladen Book B, No. 37. Thos Robeson, Clk.

Pp. 293-294: At a Superior Court held for the Dist. of Wilmington, 27 May 1770, a Judgment was secured by George Moore Exr. of the L. W. & T. of Roger Moore decd. against Thomas Rutherford, administrator of the goods & Chattles of John Dollison decd., for Ł 440 4 6 proc. money and Ł 5 5 10 for his costs, and by writ directed to James White Sheriff to levy said execution on the several tracts of land which the said John Dollison died seized of, and directed by George Moore to make title to said three tracts of land to Maurice Moore party of these presents did by indenture 27 May 1772 conveyed to said Maurice Moore, the 3 tracts land on lower side of Mine Bluff, 640 A; the other tract on the lower side of Elizabeth Dollesons land, 640 A (only two tracts mentioned) 28 May 1772. M. Moore (Seal), Wit: None. Ack. in open

1738-1779

court before Richard Henderson, 28 May 1772.

Pp. 294-295: 5 Aug 1771, James Sims Senr of Bladen Co., planter, to Jesse Carver of Cumberland Co., planter, for ₤ 15 proc. money, land on SW side of the North west River where Gromes(?) formerly lived, granted 6 March 1759...James Sims (Seal), Wit: Samuel Hollingsworth, Sampson Carver. Feby Court 1773, prov. in open Court by Samuel Hollingsworth. Maturin Colvill, C. C.

Pp. 296-297: 23 Apr 1771, Jesse Newbury of Bladen Co., planter, & wife Deborah to James & John Carver of Cumberland Co., for ₤ 10 proc. money...land on upper side of Asbus Creek on Jillisey(?) Meadow adj. Sims upper line, 200 A granted 22 Dec 1768...Jesse Newburry (Seal), Deborah Newburry (Seal), Wit: Sam Hollingsworth, Saml Carver. Feby Court 1773, prov. by Samuel Hollingsworth. Maturin Colvill, C. C.

Pp. 297-298: _____ 1767, Robt Green of Parish of Prince George in the Prov. of South Carolina, to Zachariah Smith in Bladen Co., N. C., Brother in law, to the said Robert Green, for natural love and affection and s 35...land on _____ Marsh, 300 A adj. James Balden, John Green...Robert Green (Seal), Wit: A. Green, Anthy Mitchell. Prov. by Amg Green, 9 Dec 1768. M. Moore.

Pp. 298-299: Thomas Mims and Grace Mims of Bladen Co., for ₤ 5 proc. money to William Barefeett of Bladen Co., Blacksmith, 100 A on E side of White Marsh...4 Feb 1772. Thomas Mims (Seal), Grace Mims (Seal), Wit: John Green, David Mims. Feby Court 1772, Ack. in open court by Thomas Mims & wife. Maturin Colvill, C. C.

Pp. 299-300: James Lowery of Bladen Co., planter, for ₤ 21 proc. money, to Christian Millan, land on the Mill prong of Raft Swamp, granted by patent 11 Dec 1770, 100 A; 29 Jan 1773. James Lowery (Seal), Wit: John Gilchrist, Daniel Smith. Feby Term 1773, prov. by John Gilchrist. Maturin Colvill, C. C.

Pp. 300-301: 24 Aug 1772, John ADare and Jogee his wife of Bladen Co., to John White Schoolmaster of same, for s 10 proc. money...land on SW side of the NW Branch of Cape Fear River, adj. Isaac Jones line, adj. the main road, toward John Adares house...John ADare (Seal), Joyce ADare (Seal), Wit: John Porter, A. Harvey. Prov. by John Porter, Nov. Court 1772. Maturin Colvill, C. C.

Pp. 301-302: 1 July 1767, John Smith Senr of Bladen Co., planter, to Alexander McDaniel of same, planter, for ₤ 7 proc. money...land on Buck Horn Swamp including the lower improvement granted 22 Oct 1762...John Smith (Seal), wit: Thomas Butler, Richd Elwell. Prov. Nov Term (no year given) by Richd Elwell. Maturin Colvill, C. C.

Pp. 302-303: Jacob Pitman of Bladen Co., N. C., for ₤ 30 proc. money, to James Johnston Jr., planter, land on E side Drowning Creek, adj. Oxendines corner, 200 A granted 6 May 1760...14 July 1770. Jacob Pitman (Seal), Wit: John Carsey, Ben Odom (X). August Court 1772, Prov. by Benjamin Odom. Maturin Colvill, C. C.

Pp. 303-304: 29 Jan 1772, Goen Morgan of Anson Co., planter, to

1738-1779

James Johnston of co. afsd., for ₤ 26 proc. money...land in Bladen Co., adj. Charles Oxendines improvement, granted 28 Apr 1768... Goen Morgan (Seal), Wit: Ben Odom, Wm Smith. Prov. Aug Court 1772, by Benja. Odom. Maturin Colvill, C. C.

Pp. 305-306: 28 Dec 1769, Isom Carver of Cumberland Co., N. C., and wife Betsey, to Thomas Greer of Cumberland Co., planter, by grant dated 12 Sept 1745 to Zebulon Clayton, 700 A, on Sw side of the North west River in Bladen Co., adj. lands of the late William Carver, and Richard Elwell, and the said Zebulon Clayton by deed conveyed unto Richard Bracewell the upper part of said land, adj. William Carver, and by said Richard Bracewell to John Holton, and by John Holton sold to Robert Carver, father of the said Isom Carver, and said Robert Carver in his last will and testament devised to said Isam Carver, and Zebulon Clayton sold the other part of said 700 A to Alexander Legg 14 Oct 1754, and conveyed to David Bracewell now deceased, and by his will devised to said Isom Carver, now sold to Thomas Greer and John Walsh...Isom Carver (Seal), Betsey Carver (Seal), Wit: Robert Vernor, Joseph Green. August Court 1772, prov. by Robert Vernor. Maturin Colvill, C. C.

Pp. 306-307: Thomas Brown of Bladen Co., for ₤ 50 proc. money to William Taylor...50 A on said side of Ashpole Swamp on Gumping Gully, granted to Isaac Odom 1 July 1758, conveyed to Jos Scripps then to William thence from Allen to Thomas Brown (chain of title not clear)...9 Apr 1771. Thomas Brown (Seal), Wit: Josiah Taylor, Jonathan Taylor. Nov Court 1771, prov. by Josiah Taylor. Maturin Colvill, C. C.

Pp. 308-309: 31 Oct 1772, Jesse Pitman, Planter, of Bladen Co., & wife Rachael, to Joel Pitman of same, for ₤ 10 proc. money...100 A on Hog Swamp east of Ashpole, granted 4 May 1769...Jesse Pitman (Seal), Rachael Pitman (Seal), Wit: Danl Willis, Lott Pitman. Nov. 1772, Bladen Infr. Court, prov. by Danl Willis. Maturin Colvill, C. C.

Pp. 309-310: 4 Apr 1772, Daniel Willis, planter, of Bladen Co., to Thomas Rowland, planter of same, for ₤ 40 proc. money...200 A on Idian (sic) swamp, patent dated 4 May 1769... Danl Willis (Seal), Wit: John Rowland, James Rowland. Nov. Court, 1772, prov., ack. in open court. Maturin Colvill, C. C.

Pp. 311-312: 22 Aug 1772, Nathan Horn, planter, of Bladen Co., to John Rowland, planter, of Rowan Co., for ₤ 55 proc. money...land on Ashpole or Tadpole swamp, adj. Richd Barefield, 1/2 mile about the mouth of Hog Swamp, patent dated 16 Dec 1769 ...Nathan Horn (Seal), Wit: Danl Willis, James Rowland. Nov. 1772 Bladen Indr. Court. prov. by Danl Willis. Maturin Colvill, C. C.

Pp. 312-313: 13 Oct 1772, Howell Holleman of Bladen Co., to John Smith Senr., planter, for ₤ 30 proc. money...400 A in Bladen Co., on SW side Drowning Creek, patent dated 18 Nov 177 just above Iveys Bluff landing...Howell Holleman (Seal), Wit: Danl Willis, George Willis. Prov. Nov. 1772, Bladen Infr Court, by Daniel Willis. Maturin Colvill, C. C.

Pp. 313-314: 4 Aug 1772, Phillip Ichner of Bladen Co., & wife Catherine to Lewis Munroe, planter, for ₤ 65 proc. money...land on N side Rockfish Creek, 100 A granted to Henry

1738-1779

Messer, 26 Nov 1737, also another tract granted to John McMuth 4 May 1769, on a small creek on the upper side of Rockfish adj. Counsels lower corner, 100 A...Phillip Egner (Seal), Catharine Ikner (Seal), Wit: John Legitt, Thos Davis. Nov. Term 1772. prov. by John Legett. Maturin Colvill, C. C.

Pp. 315-316: 13 July 1772, Hugh Brown of N. C., planter, to Neill Brown, Taylor, for L 60 proc. money...land on a branch the south side of the Raft Swamp, granted 8 Oct 1748, and by a deed from James Oberry to Solomon Johnston and by a deed from Solomon Johnston to Hugh Brown...Hugh Brown (Seal), Wit: Malcom Brice, Henry Smith. Bladen Co., August Court 1772, prov. by Malcom Brice. Maturin Colvill, C. C.

Pp. 316-317: 3 Oct 1771, Solomon Johnston of Parish of St. Mathew in the Prov. of Georgia, to Hugh Brown of Bladen Co., N. C., for L 60 proc. money...land on S side Raft Swamp, part of 600 A granted to Henry Oberry 8 Oct 1748, and by deed from James Oberry to Solomon Johnston...Solomon Johnston (Seal), Wit: Thomas Kersey, James Oberry, Thomas Meacham. Bladen Co., Nov. Court 1771, prov. by Thomas Caraway. Maturin Colville, C. C.

Pp. 317-318: 14 July 1772, Joseph Fort of Bladen Co., planter, to Hugh Brown, planter, for L 20 proc. money...land on Tadors Marsh S W of the Raft Swamp, between the improvements called Tadors south of said marsh...Joseph Fort (Seal), Wit: Malcom Brice, Henry Smith. Prov. August Court 1772, by Malcom Brice. Maturin Colvill, C. C.

Pp. 318-319: 24 Apr 1759, Isham Hendon of Bladen Co., to William Hendon of same, for L 35 proc. money...land on SW side of the Northwest River on Browns Creek, 245 A, one half of the tract where the said Isham Hendon now lives, adj. Davis line ...Isham Hendon (Seal), Wit: Josiah Hendon, William Singletary. Prov. April Court 1759, by Josiah Hendon. John Burgwin, C. C. Registered in the Refisteres office in Bladen County in Book C(?), folo 80.

Page 320: Josiah Taylor of Bladen Co., for L 60 proc. money to Richard Grantham of same, planter, 200 A on S side Ashpole Swamp, adj. Connoway Oateses corner, part of a larger tract granted Richard Barefield, concluding the plantation whereon Richard Grantham now lives...12 May 1771. Josiah Taylor (Seal), Wit: William Grantham, John Grantham, Joseph Oates. Ack. in open court Nov Court 1772. Maturin Colvill, C. C.

Page 321: 15 March 1770, John White of Bladen Co., planter, to John White Junr for L 150 proc. money...1/2 the stream or creek runing throu Hollinsworths land, with 1/2 of grist and saw Mill with half the Timber on Hollingsworths land with half the timber on Dennis Collins land, on the lower side of Robt McRees land, 320 A...John White (Seal), Wit: Alexr Harvey, Griffith Jones White, David Lenzy White. Prov. May Court 1770 by Griffith Jones White. Maturin Colvill, C. C.

Pp. 321-323: 19 Dec 1766, Joseph Clarke of Bladen Co., planter, to James Stuart of same, planter, for L 220 proc. money, 292 A on SW side of the Northwest branch of Cape Fear River adj. lands called and known by the name of Lisbon Gentlemens land part of 600 A granted to John Clayton 19 May 1735, and

33

1738-1779

by him conveyed over by an Indorsement on the back of said patent bearing date 12 Aug 1736, for 584 A, to John Dubois, and by Dubois conveyed to John Jones, 31 Jan 1760, and by John Jones & wife Ann to Joseph Clarke, 24 Sept 1764...Jos. Clarke (Seal), wit: Pat Stuart, Peter Broades. Prov. by William McRee, Nov Court 1772 whose swore to the hand writing of Joseph Clarke. Maturin Colvill, C. C.

Pp. 323-325: 21 Dec 1765, John Leonard of the Township of upper freehold and county of Monsmouth, Prov. of West New Jersey to Benjamin Stone of Brunswick Co., N. C., shipwirght, for ₤ 100 current money of west Jersey, land on NE side of the n W branch of Cape Fear River adj. land formerly belonging to James Boone, land formerly belonging to edward Randolph Junr, granted to Edward Fitzrandolph 20 Feb 1735, conveyed by an assignment of said patent to Thos Leonard 1 July 1737, and said Thomas Leonard bequeathed by will Recorded in the Secretaries office in Porth amboy to the above said John Leonard...Jno Leonard (Seal), Wit: John Brown, John Toreman Harriet, Wm Stone. Certificate from Jonathan Deare notary public in Porth Amboy, New Jersey, that the deed was proved by William Stone, in Middlesex Co., N. J., 19 July 1770. Prov. before Stephen Skinner.

Page 326: N. C., Bladen County: William Shinglton & wife Mary, doth sell in open market to Robert Sims, 100 A on the Raft Swamp where Moses Bas(?) old Mill was as so called ...12 Nov 1766, for ₤ 10 proc. money...William Shinglton (Seal), Mary Shinglton (Seal), Wit: John Jones. Prov. by John Jones, Nov. 24 1772, M. Moore.

Pp. 327-328: N. C., Bladen Co.: James McDaniel, planter, & wife Agnus, for ₤ 200 proc. money to Samuel Butler, of same, blacksmith...the upper part of 640 A granted 16 Nov 1764 adj. Jesse Newbury, 145 A...24 Aug 1771. James McDaniel, Agness McDaniel (Seal), Wit: Nathaniel Reeves, Michael Easlace. Ack. in open Court, Novr. Court 1771.

Pp. 328-329: 29 May 1749, John Malsby of Bladen Co., planter, & wife Mary, to William Maulsby, son of said John and Mary Maulsby, for natural love & affection...300 A in Bladen Co., on SW side of NW River and on the head of Hammons Creek, land granted to him 1735, 13 Sept....John Maulsby (Seal), Mary Maulsby (Seal), Wit: Saml Carver, Juren Rools, Jas. Carver. Rec. in open court June 1749 by oath of Jurin Rools. Thos Robeson, clk. Registered in C, folo 98, July 6th 1749. Thos Robeson, Regr.

Pp. 329-330: N. C., Bladen County: John Stevens & wife Sarah of Cumberland Co., for ₤ 30...to Joseph Thumbs, tract patented by Henry Sims, 1753, conveyed to John Stevens, adj. Grays, Danns, 40 A...15 Nov 1776. John Stevens (Seal), Sarah Stevens (Seal), Wit: John Beard, Joseph Thumbs, Joseph White. N. C., Bladen County, Novr Court 1772, ack. in open court. Maturin Colvill, C. C.

Pp. 331-332: 25 Aug 1772, Samuel Carman of Bladen Co., Shingle maker, to William Johnson of rsame, for ₤ 100 proc. money...640 A, on the White Oak swamp west of Ellyses Creek swamp granted 18 Nov 1771; also 100 A on Cedar Swamp granted May 1772... Samuel Carman (Seal), Wit: John Richuson, James Johnson, Elizabeth Johnson. Prov. by John Richardson, Feb. Court 1772.

1738-1779

Page 332: Joseph Price administrator of Stephen Shepard deceased
of Bladen Co., appoint Silvanus Wilson of Cumberland
Co., my lawful attorney, to collect debts now due to Stephen
Shepard decd...4 Feb 1773. Joseph Price (Seal), Wit: James McDaniel. Prov. Feby court 1773, ack. in open court. Maturin Colvill,
C. C.

Pp. 333-334: 28 Nov 1743, William White of Newhanover co., Millwright, to William Bartram of Bladen Co., carpenter,
for ₺ 600 current money of sd. prov...land on NE side of the River
opposite to where Ralph Miller now liveth, between lands of George
Martin, Dr. Thomas Halt...Willm White (Seal), Wit: Nathl Pigott.
George Brown. March Court 1743/4 prov. by George Brown. Jno
Clayton, C. C. Registered April 19th 1744, folio 405.

Pp. 334-335: 19 March 1750, William Bartram to Anthony Golley
both of Anson County, 300 A more or less on the NE
side of the River opposite to where Ralph Miller lived, between
lands granted for George Martin and Thomas Hall...Willm Bartram
(Seal), Wit: John Jones, Jno Evans. Ack. in court March 1753 by
William Bartrom. Reg. in Book D, folio No. 95., Apl 2, 1753. Thos
Robeson, Regr.

Pp. 335-336: John Davis of precinct of Bladen, Esqr., for ₺ 5 to
William White, of same, planter, 291 A on NE side
of the River adj. Thomas Hall, George Martin...18 March 1737/8.
Jno Davis (Seal), Wit: Wm Forbes, John Dallison. Sepr Court 1738,
Prov. by Wm Forbes, Esqr. Richd. Halleor, Clk Cor.

Page 336: William Moore of Bladen Co., for love and good will to
the Worship of Almighty God, to Baptist Society holding
believers Baptism, Final Perservance, Person Election & Eternal
redemption, two acres on NE of the NW Branch of Cape Fear River,
part of a grant to John Brown 19th June 1736...1 Dec 1759. William
Moore (Seal), Wit: Benjamin Singletary, Thos Vance. Prov. May
Court 1761, by Benjamin Singletary. Jno Burgwin, C. C. Reg. in
Book E, folio 148.

Pp. 337-338: 11 Oct 1766, John Legett and wife Rachael of Bladen
Co., carpenter, to James Jackson for ₺ 100...220 A
part of grant to John Dunn, conveyed to Richard Dunn Senior,
then to Robt Dun, and to Thomas Thumbs senior, and after his
decease to his children...John Legett (Seal), Rachael Legett (Seal),
Wit: Silvanus, Wilson, Jesse Newbury. Bladen Novr court 1768,
Prov. by Jesse Newbury, Arthur Howe.

Pp. 338-339: 29 Oct 1768, James Jackson & Marshea his wife of Cumberland Co., to William Maulsby, Carpenter, of same,
for ₺ 150...land in Bladen Co., on SW side of the NW River of
Cape Fear, patented for Richud Dunn Senr, 220 A, granted to John
Dunn, conveyed to Richard Dunn senr, to Robt Dunn, to Thomas
Thumbs senr and by his last will & Testament left the same to his
sons John & Amos Thumbs, and by them to John Legett, then to
James Jackson...James Jackson (Seal), Marshea Jackson (Seal), Wit:
Edmeston Wir, George Evans. Bladen Novr Court 1768, prov. by
Edmiston Wire. Arthur Howe, Cler Cor.

Pp. 339-340: 30 Apr 1739, Joseph Plummer of Bladen Prect. planter,
to William Bartram, of same, carpenter, for ₺ 200...
250 A on NE side of the River opposite to Swanns Creek, adj.
William Masons...Joseph Plummer (Seal), Eliphe Plummer (Seal),

35

1738-1779

Wit: Thos Lock, John Gervis. Bladen Co., N. C., June Court 1739. Ack in open court. Richd. Hellur, C. C. Reg. July the 20th 1739.

Pp. 340-341: William Sims & Margaret Sims of Craven Co., South Carolina, for ₺ 200 proc. money to James McDaniel of Bladen Co., planter, 200 A on NE side of the NW River part of a grant to William Gray, for 350 A, allotted by said William Gray in his last Dividend of land to his daughter Margaret wife of the aforesaid William Sims...4 Aug 1769. Wm Sims (Seal), Margaret Sims (Seal), Wit: Silvanus Wilson, Joseph Cooper, Benja. Cooper. August Court 1771, prov. in open Court by Joseph Cooper. Maturin Colvill, C. C.

Pp. 341-342: 20 May 1772, James Stewart of Bladen Co., planter, to Morgan Drewry of same, planter, for ₺ 30 proc. money...land on W side of the NW River on Raft Swamp, granted 31 March 1755...James Swart (sic) (Seal), Wit: John Wilson, Thomas Ard. Nov. Court 1772, prov. by Thomas Ard. Maturin Colvill, C. C.

Pp. 343-344: 5 Aug 1771, William Singleton of Bladen Co., and wife Mary, to James Stewart, for ₺ 30 proc. money... land on W side of NW River on the Raft Swamp, patent dated 31 March 1755...William Singleton (Seal), Mary Singleton (Seal), Wit: John Blount, Archd. McKissack. Prov. Feb. Court 1772, by Archd. Mc. Maturin Colvill, C. C.

Pp. 344-346: 14 Oct 1769, Joseph Cooper of Bladen Co., & wife Mary and Benjamin Cooper of same, planter, to Leonard Lock of Cumberland Co., for ₺ 200 proc. money...land on SW side of NW River between a piece of land patented by Henry Sims 400 A, patented in the name of David Morley, 80 A granted to David Morley 23 Nov 1744, conveyed to Benjam. Elwell, then to Wm. Newbury, then to Benjamin Cooper, and conveyed by him to his two sons Benjamin and Joseph Cooper; also another tract on SW side of NW River between Espies Creek and the above land patented in the name of David Morley, 100 A granted to Henry Sims 16 June 1736, conveyed to Benja Elwell, then to William Newburry, then to Benjamin Cooper, then to Benja & Joseph Cooper...Joseph Cooper (Seal), Mary Cooper (Seal), Benja. Cooper (Seal), Wit: John Leggett, Richard Willkison. Prov. by John Legett, Nov. Term 1772. Maturin Colvill, C. C.

Pp. 347-348: 19 Jan 1773, Silvanus Wilson of Cumberland Co., and wife Rebecca, to William Anderson of Bladen Co., for ₺ 40 proc. money...land on NE side of NW River adj. John Sincombs land, 160 A...Silvanus Wilson (Seal), Rebekkah Wilson (Seal), Wit: Archibald McDaniel, Robert Wilson, Bladen Feby Court 1772. Prov. by Archibald McDaniel. Maturin Colvill, C. C.

Pp. 348-349: 24 Dec 1773, Isaac Kenady of Bladen Co., planter, to George Ikener of same, for ₺ 20 s 10 proc. money... land west of the great Marsh, ¼ mile below Jones's path, 100 A patented 18 Nov 1771...Isaac Kenady (Seal), Wit: Absalom Legett, John Legett. May Court 1774, by John Legett prov. Alfred Moore, C. C.

Pp. 349-351: 30 Dec 1773, John Branch of Bladen Co., planter, to Archibald Black of Cumberland Co., for ₺ 30 proc. money...land on NE of Drowning Creek, 50 A, patent 22 Dec 1770, No. 185, adj. Solomon Johnston, Archibald Smith, line made in

1738-1779

John Branch and Beslon Branch, granted to Solomon Johnston 23 Dec 1768, conveyed from Johnston to John McCraney, then to John Branch, then to Archibald Black...John Branch (Seal), Wit: Phillip Ivekner, John Leggett. Prov. by John Leggett, May Court 1774. Alfred Moore, C.

Pp. 351-352: 23 Apr 1774, John Legett of Bladen Co., to Absalom Legett of same, for Ł 20 proc. money...200 A on a branch east of the great Marsh, adj. John Gill, granted May 1773 ...John Legett (Seal), Wit: James Biggs, Benjamin Britt. Ack. by John Legett, May Court 1774. Alfred Moore, C. C.

Pp. 353-354: 7 Apr 1774, John Legett and Isaiah Powell of Bladen Co., to Absalom Legett of same, for Ł 30 proc. money ...land on a brach of the Big Marsh called the Gum Branch, 100 A granted 3 May 1760 to John Gill and conveyed by Deed to John Jones & conveyed from Jones to Isaiah Powell, and conveyed by Powell to John Legett...John Legett (Seal), Isaiah Powell (Seal) Wit: James Beggs, Benjamin Brett. Prov. May Court 1774 by James Biggs. Alfred Moore, C. C.

Pp. 354-355: 23 Apr 1774, Thos Davis of Bladen Co., to James Biggs of same, for Ł 15 proc. money...land on a branch of Pughs little (sic) adj. Hector McNeill, granted May 1773... Thomas Davis (Seal), Wit: Absalom Legett, William Herbird. Prov. by Absalom Legett, May Court 1774. Alfred Moore, C. C.

Pp. 355-356: William Gulledge of Bladen Co., planter, for Ł 50 proc. money to Roger McGill of same, land on E side Drowning Creek, adj. to a survey formerly made by John Bates(?), granted to Robert Edwards, 23 May 1772, 100 A...8 Apr 1774. William Gulledge (Seal), Wit: John Gilchrist, John Watson. Prov. May Court 1774, by John Gilchrist. Alfred Moore, C. C.

Pp. 356-357: N. C. Bladen County: Lisha Sweeten planter, for Ł 8 proc. money pd. by John McMillan Dugald McMillan Eldest son at present in Cumberland co., prov. aforesaid, land on SW side Drowning Creek, about 2 miles below Thomas Robisons survey, 50 A...22 Dec 1773. Lisha Sweeten (Seal), Wit: John Gilchrist, John McCrainey. Prov. May Court 1774, by John Gilchrist. Alfred Moore, C. C.

Pp. 357-358: N. C., Bladen Co., Abraham Strickland of co. afsd., to John Watson, for Ł 20 proc. money...200 A on the east edge of Drowning Creek about ¼ mile above the mouth of long Swamp...2 July 1773. Abraham Strickland (Seal), Martha Strickland. Wit: Malcom Mcfater, William Gulledge, John Gilchrist. May Court 1774, prov. by John Gilchrist. Alfred Moore, C. C.

Pp. 358-359: N. C., Bladen Co., for Ł 46 proc. money to John McNear...150 A, the lower part of a tract of 640 A granted to Richd Smith, Dec. 22, 1768, and by said Richd Smith, 300 A conveyed to me by a deed of sale...8 Jany 1774. Moses Grice (Seal), Mary Grice (Seal), Wit: John Gilchrist, John C--ly. Prov. by John Gilchrist, Alfred Moore, C. C., May Court 1774.

Page 360: N. C. Bladen Co., Moses Grice for Ł 22 s 5 proc. money to Daniel McNear, 150 A, the upper part of 300 A conveyed by deed from Richard Smith...15 Jan 1774. Moses Grice (Seal) Mary Grice (Seal), Wit: John Gilchrist, John Felveg(?). Prov. May Court 1774 by John Gilchrist; Alfred Moore, C. C.

1738-1779

Page 361: 13 Oct 1773, William Gibson, James White, James Bailey & Benja. Humphreys, Directors for the Town of Elizabeth, to William Sattur of Bladen Co., for ₺ 10 proc. money...½ A lot, in Elizabeth Town, numbered 44...Walter Gibson (Seal), James Bailey (Seal), James White (Seal), Benja. Humphres (Seal), Wit: Wm McRee, Ithamer Singletary. Prov. by Willm. McRee, Augt Term 1774. Alfred Moore, C. C.

Pp. 361-363: 2 Apr 1759, Francis Parker of Bladen Co., planter, to John Lucas of same, planter, for ₺ 20 proc. money ...land on SW side of the NW River, 250 A, ½ of 500 A granted to sd. Francis Parker 25 Feb 1754, adj. John Lucas, William Clemmond ...Francis Parker (Seal), Tabitha Parker (Seal), Wit: Richd Mallington, Jos Clarke. Rec. 2 Apr 1759, receipt. 8 June 1753, Tabitha Parker relinquished dower before Jas. Hassell, C. J. Registered in Book E, Folio 227. J. Burgwin, Regr. May Court 1774 Ordered to be Registered. Alfred Moore, C. C.
(It would appear that this deed was recorded twice, by the above notations.)

Page 364: Isaac Woolf of Bladen Co., for ₺ 33 proc. money to Simon Green of prov. afsd., planter, land on N side of the Western prong, adj. Mr. Adams...4 Sept 1773. Isaac Woolf. Wit: John Green, William Green. Prov. by John Green (no date) Alfred Moore, C. C.

Pp. 364-366: 4 Sept 1773, Joseph Howard of Bladen Co., planter, and wife Sarah, to Robert Stewart of same, planter, for ₺ 100 proc. money...150 A adj. Vernons Corner, by the River Swamp, 150 A excepted to his son William Howard, by deed 21 Oct 1758, and 50 A more taken out by deed made 1759, patent bearing date 10 May 1753...Joseph Howard (Seal), Sarah Howard (Seal), Wit: _____ Funt (German signature), Othniel Stratram. Prov. by Othniel Strahan, Alfred Moore, C. C. (no date)

Pp. 366-367: 4 Sept 1773, Joseph Howard of Bladen Co., planter & wife Sarah, to Robert Stewart, for ₺ 100 proc. money ...300 A on E side of Colleys Swamp at a place called Turkey point, patented 6 Apr 1765...Joseph Howard (Seal), Sarah Howard (Seal), Cresswell Hunt, Othniel Straham. Prov. by Strahan, May Term 1774. Alfred Moore, C. C.

Pp. 367-369: 10 Apr 1773, Jeremiah Begford, cemur(?), and wife Magdalene of Bladen Co., planter, to John Kelly of same, for ₺ 30 proc. money...200 A, part of a grant to Jeremiah Begford, and conveyed to John Kelly, the upper part of 300 A, between Captain Campbells and the widow Comer(?)...Jeremiah Begford (Seal), Magdaleen Begford (Seal), Wit: William Bryan, James Lewis. Prov. by James Lewis, Alfred Moore, C. C. (no date)

Pp. 369-370: James Wilkeson of Bladen Co., planter, for ₺ 40 proc. money, to Hector McLean, Labrough (sic), 100 A on a branch of Little Pedee, granted to William M----, 24 Aug 1767... James Wilkeson (Seal), Wit: Jno Cade, Archd. McKissak. Prov. by oath of John Cade. Alfred Moore, C. C. (no date).

Page 370: 28 Jan 1773, John Ballard of Bladen Co., to Gilbert McCarmag of same, for ₺ 30 proc. money...100 A on a prong of little Pedee, granted to John Ballard, 10 Apr 1761...John Ballard (Seal), Elizabeth Hobson Cade, Wit: Richd Smith, John Cade. Prov. by John McCarnag. Ordered to be Registered, Alfred

1738-1779

Moore, C. C.

Pp. 373-374: 23 March 1773, Benjamin Fuller of prov. of South Carolina to James Adair of Dobbs County, N. C., for Ł 20 proc. money...200 A in Bladen Co., on both sides of Wilkesons Swamp, east of little Pedee...Benjamin Fuller (Seal), Wit: John Cade, Edward Hughs. Prov. by John Cade. Alfred Moore, C. C. (no date).

Pp. 374-375: 2 May 1774, Peter Byrne of Bladen Co., to Benjamin Clarke, planter, of same, for Ł 60 proc. money... 103 A on NE side of the N. W. River adj. John Forester, being part of a tract sold by John Forester to James Moorehead deceased, then John King marrying Jane Moorehead daughter to the sd. James, the said 103 A became and then the said John King sold 103 A to Peter Byrne...Peter Byrne (Seal), Wit: Lawrence Byrne, Matthew Byrne. Ack. in court & ordered to be registered. Alfred Moore, C. C.

Pp. 375-376: N. C, Bladen County: Neill McFall of co. afsd., planter, for Ł 12 proc. money, to Neill Brown, planter, of same...land on a branch of the Raft Swamp, granted 20 May 1770, 50 A...below Ann Perkins survey, Neill McFall, Wit: Alexr Makay, Hugh Brown. Prov. by Hugh Brown, (no date). Alfred Moore, Clk.

Pp. 376-377: 3 Dec 1773, Jacob Pitman of Bladen Co., planter, to Hugh McCrane, planter, of same, for Ł 20 proc. money ...100 A on Burnt Swamp west of the raft Swamp, surveyed for Jacob Pitman 5 Apr 1771...Jacob Pitman (Seal), N Cannah Pitman (Seal), Wit: Hugh Brown, John Jackson. Prov. by Hugh Brown, Alfred Moore, C. C. (no date).

Pp. 377-378: Nathaniel Sanders for Ł 5 proc. money to Hector McNeill, Sailor...land granted Dec 1768, 100 A, a little above Sizemores old field...10 Dec 1773. Nathaniel Sanders (Seal), Wit: An McPoumecy, Daniel Smith. Prov. by Daniel Smith, Alfred Moore, Clk. (no date).

Pp. 378-379: Moses Russ of South Carolina, for Ł 15 proc. money to Malcolm Brice, planter, 100 A on E side Solomons Swamp, including where Thomas Dugers (Drugers?) lived...15 Nov 1772. Moses Russ (Seal), Wit: Thomas Consey, Jas. Simpson. Prov. by Daniel Smith, (sic), Alfred Moore, Clk.

Pp. 379-380: 31 July 1773, Nathaniel Sanders of South Carolina to Daniel Smith of Bladen Co., for Ł 10 proc. money, land on Solomons Swamp east of Drowning Creek, 100 A... Nathaniel Sanders (Seal), Wit: An McPouncy, Hector McNeal. Prov. by Hector McNeal, Alfred Moore, Clk.

Pp. 380-381: Francis Lucus & wife Elizabeth of Bladen Co., for Ł60 proc. money to Samuel Rhuark of same, land on E side of White Marsh, 100 A, granted to Joseph Pye 27 Feb 1735, conveyed to said Galloway by deed 23 Feb 1737, and to James Lyon Esqr by deed 22 Feb 1742, and the said James Lyon by his last will and Testament to his daughter Elizabeth Lyon, now Elizabeth Lucus...5 Jan 1773. Francis Lucas (Seal), Elizabeth Lucas (Seal), Wit: George Lyon, James Carver. Prov. by George Lyon May Term 1774. Alfred Moore, Clk.

1738-1779

Pp. 382-383: 4 Sept 1767, Hugh Rae of Cumberland Co., N. C., & wife Catharine, to John McDuffee of Bladen co., planter, for Ł 40 proc. money...land on the Brown Marsh Swamp, 306 A granted by pattent to James Waltham, conveyed to him by Richd Quince, and since conveyed from Quince to John McCauslin, from John McCauslin to Daniel McKeithan, then to Hugh Rae, Registered in the Registers office for Bladen Co., Book E, folio 169, 13 Aug 1761, adj. Sarah Graves land, half of 612 A...Hugh Rae (Seal), Catharin Rae (Seal), Wit: Archibald Shaw, Malcom buie. Prov. by Shaw, May Term 1774. Alfred Moore, Clk.

Pp. 383-384: 7 Feb 1774, Dougald McDuffee of Bladen Co., to Dougald Blue of same, planter, for Ł 50 proc. money...land on Brown Morsh Swamp, 306 A, 18 or 20 already assigned to Duncan McKeithan, part of 612 A granted to James Walton, conveyed to Richard Quince, then to John McCauslin, to Daniel McKeithan, to Hugh Rae and from Hugh Rae to Dugald McDuffee...Dugald McDuffee (Seal), Wit: Wm. McNutt (McNull?), Alexander Shaw, Gillr. McKeithan. Prov. by Shaw. Alfred Moore, Clk.

Pp. 385-386: 27 Jan 1761, Thomas White of Bladen Co., Mill Right, to William Howe of same, planter, for Ł 25 proc. money....land on SW side of the North West River on a branch of Hannons Creek between Thomas Whites home place & James Campbells land, granted to Whomas White 21 Oct 1758...Thomas White (Seal), Wit: Chas. Stevens, Richd Mallington. Feb. Court 1761, prov. by Richard Mallington. J. Burgwin, C. C. Reg. in Book E, folio 131.

Pp. 386-387: 2 May 1774, Moses Coleman of Bladen Co., planter, to John Coleman, of same, planter, for Ł 5 proc. money ...land on E side Drowning Creek on both sides of a branch that runs through John Willis old Survey, 200 A...Moses Coleman (Seal) Wit: Coleman Nichols, William Strickland. Prov. by Coleman Nichols, May Term 1774. Alfred Moore, C. C.

Pp. 387-388: 25 Oct 1773, Isham Hatcher of Bladen co., to John Coleman, of same, for Ł 40 proc. money...land on S side Drowning Creek on Cabbages Swamp, 140 A, part of 640 A granted to John Willis...Isham Hatcher (LS), Wit: James Brown, Thos Horn, Isaac Hatcher. Prov. by James Brown, May Term 1774. Alfred Moore, C.

Page 389: N. C., Bladen County: 17 Dec 1772, James Grantham of co. afsd., planter, to Dempsey Dawson of Edgecomb Co., for Ł 50 proc. money...land on S side of Cabbages Swamp of Drowning Creek, 150 A...James Grantham (Seal), Wit: John Coleman, Moses Coleman. Phebe Coleman. Prov. by John Coleman, Feb. Court 1773. Maturin Colvill, C. C.

Pp. 390-391: 26 Apr 1772, Phillip Ikner of Bladen co., to George Ikner, for Ł 20 proc. money...land on lower side of _____ Creek, on western side of Plotts pond, 100 A granted May 1772, Phillip Ikner (Seal), Wit: John Legett, Henry Messer. _____ (German signature). Ack in open Court. Alfred Moore, Clk. (No date).

Pp. 391-392: 28 June 1774, Phillip Ikner of Bladen Co., to Michael Ikner of same, for Ł 40 proc. money...land on N side Pughs little Marsh, 100 A, granted 13 Nov 1753, the place where Oxentine formerly lived, conveyed to Thomas Tail, of John County, then to Summersit Dunohow & to George Ikner, then to Philip Ikner...Phillip Ikner (Seal), Wit: John Leggett, _____. Prov. by

40

1738-1779

John Legget, August Term 1774. Alfred Moore, Clerk.

Pp. 392-393: 1 Aug 1774, Thos Creel of Bladen Co., to Thomas Davis, for Ŀ 10 proc. money...grant to Thomas Creel July 1774, 100 A. Thomas Creel (Seal), Wit; John Legett, _____. Prov. by John Legett, August Term 1774. Alfred Moore, C. C.

Pp. 394-395: 4 Dec 1773, Samuel Kenedy of Bladen Co., planter, to Archibald Little of Cumberland Co., for Ŀ 15 proc. money...640 A on east side of Pughs little Marsh, the western corner of Kenedys survey, patent 22 May 1772...Samuel Kenedy (Seal), Wit: Absalom Leget, Alexr Hofmillon, John Legett. Prov. by John Legett, August term 1774. Alfred Moore.

Pp. 395-396: 16 May 1774, George Ikner of Bladen Co., to Joseph Price, for Ŀ 40 proc. money...land on S side Pughs Little Marsh, 100 A...George Ikner (Seal), Wit: John Legett, Phillip ____ (German signature). Prov. by John Legett, August Term 1774. Alfred Moore, Clk.

Pp. 396-397: 7 March 1772, John Legett of Bladen Co., planter, to Mary Blue, for Ŀ 14 proc. money...land on Buck horn Swamp including the lower improvement, part of tract surveyed for John Smith Senr, patent dated 22 Oct 1762...John Legett (Seal), Wit: Thos Robinson, Tobias Sealey. Ack & Ordered to be Registered August Term 1774. Alfred Moore, Clk.

Pp. 397-398: N. C. Bladen Co., Isaac Wilkes of co. afsd., planter, for Ŀ 12 proc. money, to Neal Mcfoal & Archd. McEachern, planters, land on Pedlars branch below Rockfish, granted Jan 1773, 100 A...Isaac Wilkes (Seal), Wit/ Neill Blue, Daniel McLaughlan. Prov. by McLauchlin, Alfred Moore Clk.

Pp. 399-400: N. C., Bladen Co., Isaac Wilkes of co. afsd., planter, to Donald McLauchlan, planter, of same, for Ŀ 35 proc. money...land on Gum Swamp East of Drowning Creek, a survey granted to me Jan 1773, 100 A...19 March 1774. Isaac Wilkes (Seal), Wit: Neill Blue, Archd. McEachers. Prov. by McEachers, Alfred Moore, Clk. (no date).

Pp. 400-401: 13 Oct 1773, David Young of Bladen Co., planter, to Daniel McEachern, on a branch east of the great Marsh, 100 A, granted May 1772 to John Legett, and conveyed by deed to David Young...David Young (Seal), Wit: John Legett, Benja. Powell. Ack. in open court. Alfred Moore, Clk.

Pp. 401-402: N. C., Bladen Co.: Donald Campbell of Cumberland Co., planter, to Malcolm McNeill for Ŀ 25 proc. money... land on branch of the Raft Swamp called Solomons or Richland Swamp, granted 1771, 50 A, including Daniel Moodys improvement... Donald Campbell (Seal), Wit: Archd. McEachern, Daniel McLauchlan, John Price. Prov. by Daniel McLauchlan, Alfred Clk.

Pp. 402-403: N. C. Bladen Co., David Young, planter, for Ŀ 50 proc. money to Donald McEacharn, planter, land on Gum Branch granted 2 March 1761, 100 A...David Young (Seal), Wit: John Legett, Benja. Powell. Ack. in court. Alfred Moore, Clk.

Pp. 403-404: 7 Oct 1771, Joshua Stevens of Bladen Co., to Coleman Nichols of Johnson County, for Ŀ 80 proc. money... land granted 22 Dec 1768, on E side of Drowning Creek, on Cubages

41

1738-1779

or Porters Swamp...Joshua Stevens (Seal), Wit: John Yeates, William Howe, James Grantham. Novr Court 1771, prov. by John Yeates. Maturin Colvill, C. C.

Page 405: 27 Spt 1772, John Burgwin Esqr. Merchant of New Hanover Co., to David Goodwin of Johnson Co., for Ł 50 proc. money...land on Cow branch on Drwoning Creek, patented to John Stark late of Bladen Co., and conveyed to John Burgwin, 300 A... John Burgwin (Seal), Wit: James Clardy, Thos Grahm. Prov. by James Clardy, May term 1774. Alfred Moore, C. C.

Pp. 406-407: 7 July 1774, Francis Bottis of Craven County, St. Marks Parish, South Carolina, to Archibald Campbell of Cumberland Co., planter, for Ł 135 proc. money...640 A on E side Drowning Creek about a mile below the old ford, granted 6 Apr 1750 to John Davis, and by him assigned to said Bottis by deed, Registered in the Registers office of Cumberland County, dated 16 Aug 1759...Francis Bottis (Seal), Wit: Francis Bottis Junr., Hugh Campbell. Prov. by Hugh Campbell. Alfred Moore, C. C.

Pp. 407-408: 1 Dec 1772, Robert Francis of New Hanover Co., Hatter, to John Connelly of Bladen Co., for Ł 20 proc. money...400 A granted by Gov. Gabriel Johnson to Samuel Thornton, and conveyed to Bryan Corner, and conveyed by Elender Conner (his widdow) then being proper heir to it to Thomas Rook by a deed 27 Nov 1763, Reg. in Book E, adj. Ralph Milars...Robert Francis (Seal), Wit: Geo. Gibbs, James White. Prov. by James White. Alfred Moore, Clk.

Page 408: N. C. Bladen County: Mrs. Elizabeth Richardson at the request of Ralph Miller Junr made oath before me on the Holy Evangelist...that about Twenty four or Twenty five years ago or perhaps longer her husband Ralph Ben Young sold Ralph Miller a Tract of land which is the land that Ralph Miller Junr lives on as she is told & that the said Miller paid Value for said plantation she also says that Ralph Benyoung farther had the land of Nathaniel Rice as her husband informed her & further the deponent saith not this 4th July 1774. Elizth. Richardsoon. Wit: Thos Owen. Alfred Moore, Clk.

N. C. Bladen County: Whereas at the instance & request of Ralph Miller Jr. personally appeared Thos Robeson Senr before me Thos Owen, J. P. and made oath that when he acted as Clerk & Register of the County of Bladen Registered a Deed for 320 A conveyed by Mr. Ralph Benyoung to Ralph Miller Senr that when the said Thos Robeson acted as Sheriff of the said County he recd the Quitrents of the said Ralph Miller Senr for two years...22nd June 1774. Thos Owen. Thos Robeson Senr. Alfred Moore, Clk.

Page 409: N. C., Bladen County: Sold and delivered to John Lucas at public vendue one Negro wench named Cate & child renty for Ł 100 by order of court to raise the sum above mentioned out of the estate of Ann Vernon decd. for paying several legacies out of said Estate...20 June 1773. Thos Hester, Wit: T. Brown, Tan Chil. May Term 1774, Ack. in open court. Alfred Moore, Clk.

Pp. 409-410: 9 July 1774, George Young of Bladen Co., to John Little of same, planter, for Ł 40 current money... 100 A on the great Marsh, granted to James Stewart, and by deed from Stewart to George Young, 3 May 1760...George Young (Seal), Wit: Archd. Campbell, Archd. McEacharn. Prov. by Campbell.

42

1738-1779

Pp. 410-411: John Turner of Bladen Co., for ₤ 30 proc. money to
John Clark, of same, planter, tract granted to John Turner 16 Dec 1769, 100 A...Jno Turner (Seal), Wit: Geo Gibbs, Richd. Boyd. Ack. May Term 1774. Alfred Moore, Clk.

Pp. 411-412: Able Davis of Craven County, South Carolina, for
₤ 100 SC currency, to John Smith Senr, 640 A on S side Bogan Swamp, between the white marsh and the lake, granted to Francis David 5 June 1740...4 Dec 1773. Able Davis (Seal), Wit: Joseph Banon, Stephen Smith. Prov. by Stephen Smith, May Term 1774. Alfred Moore, Cl.

Pp. 412-413: 2 Aug 1773, Thomas Jones of Bladen Co., to Francis
Lucas of same, for ₤ 16 proc. money...land on SW side of the NW River, 150 A, part of tract belonging formerly to Thomas Davis decd, on a branch of Hammonds Creek...Thomas Jones (Seal), Wit: John Lucus, James Carver. Prov. by John Lucas, May Term 1774. Alfred Moore, C. C.

Pp. 413-414: 2 Dec 1773, Nathan Jones of Bladen Co., planter, to
George Brown of same, for ₤ 6 proc. money...part of a tract on east side Drowning Creek, on Turners branch adj. George Brown, granted to Nathaniel Busbe, 150 A, 18 May 1771, conveyed by Busbee to Nathan Jones, 30 A now sold...Nathan Jones (Seal), Wit: James Bailey, Zans. Child. Prov. by Zans. Child, Alfred Moore, Clk.

Pp. 414-415: William Howard to Othneil Strahan, land on S side
Black River, 250 A...deed of gift. 18 June 1773. William Howard (Seal), Wit: Patrick Nuton, John Curry. Prov. by Patrick Nuten, May Term 1774. Alfred Moore, C. C.

Pp. 415-416: 11 July 1774, Francis Bottis of South Carolina,
Craven County, St. Marks Parish, to John Campbell of Cumberland Co., N. C., for ₤ 20 proc. money...land in Bladen Co., formerly Cumberland, 100 A on east side Drowning Creek, adj. land he bought from William Davis, patent dated 22 Apr 1763...Francis Bottis (F) (Seal), Wit: Francis Bottis Junr, Hugh Campbell. Prov. by Hugh Campbell, Alfred Moore, Cl.

Pp. 416-417: 6 Apr 1773, Lazarus Creel of Bladen Co., to Edmund
Baxley of same, for ₤ 40 proc. money...land on Ten mile swamp, granted to Joseph Fort, 100 A, 23 Oct 1761...Lazarus Creel (Seal), Wit: John Blount, Joseph Williams. Prov. by John Blount, May Term 1774. Alfred Moore, Clk.

Pp. 418-419: 2 May 1774, Samuel Anders of Bladen Co., planter, to
George Hanell of same, for ₤ 25 proc. money...land on E side Raft Swamp, 100 A, granted 23 Oct 1761...Samuel Andrews (Seal), Wit: Samuel Edwards, Aba Andrews, Sarah Edwards. May Term 1774, Ack. in Court. Alfred Moore, C. C.

Pp. 419-420: 29 Nov 1773, Jacob Pope of Bladen Co., to Samuel
Andrews, for ₤ 6 s 10...land on five mile branch a branch of Saddle Tree Swamp, granted 1771, it being the land whereon Thomas Russel now lives...Jacob Pope (Seal), Wit: Nathl Richardson, Samuel Richardson. Prov. by Natl. Richardson, Alfred Moore, Clk.

Pp. 420-421: N. C., Bladen County: John Rogerson for ₤ 100 to
Joseph Butler...land on NE side of the NW river adj.

43

John Husbands, 120 A, granted to John Boath, 20 Feb 1735...8 Jan 1771. John Rogerson (Seal), Wit: John Beard, James Beard. Prov. by John Beard, August 1771. Maturin Colvill, C. C.

Page 421: N. C., Archd. Black of Cumberland Co., for ₺ 40 to James McNabb of Bladen Co., 100 A in Bladen Co., on Rockfish Creek above Beaver Creek...1 Feb 1773. Archd. Black (Seal), Wit: Hector McNeill, John Legett. Prov. by Hector McNeill Feby Term 1773. Maturin Colvill, C. C.

Pp. 421-422: North Carolina, Bladen County. February the 5th 1773 This Day Levi Glass came into the Grand Jury Room in presence of the Grand Jury whose names is underneath writen & declared upon his oath that he recd no Note of George Young nor Satisfaction from him for an asault as he said in a few minutes after he was turner out of the room Some of the Jurors request that he might be called in he then acknowledge on oath that he did recieve a Note for five pounds but said he thode (sic) it away some of the Jurors asked him whiy he did not give it to the man he said it was Burnt given under our hands the Day & year above writen.

       John Legett Foreman
       John Bryan
       Philemon Bryan
       Richard Harrison
       George Lyon
       Joseph Mercer
       John Blount
       Edward Davis
       Robert McConkey
       Benjamin Beasly
       John Baldwin
       Mathew Bulley
       Archd. McCoalskey
       John McCrane
       Ever McMulon
       Simon Bright
       Neill Shaw.

Recorded and Ordered to be Registered May Term 1774. Alfred Moore, C. C.

Pp. 422-423: N. C., Bladen Co., Robert Edwards for ₺ 10 proc. money, to William Gullage, land on E side of Drowning Creek, adj. survey made for John Bottis, granted May 1772...28 Dec 1772. Ro. Edwards (Seal), Wit: James Beard, Samuel Butler. Nov Term 1774, Ack. in open court. Alfred Moore, Clk.

Pp. 423-424: N. C. Bladen Co.: Daniel McDaniel of Edgecomb Co., for ₺ 6 proc. money to Samuel Butler, Blacksmith of Bladen Co., 200 A on NE side of NW River, on the head of James Creek, granted 1767, 5 Oct to Samuel Butler and Daniel McDaniel in copartnership...10 Oct 1774. Daniel Mc Daniel (Seal), Wit: Robert Edwards, Ann Edwards. Novr Term 1774, prov. by Robert Edwards, Alfred Moore, Clk.

Pp. 424-425: Caroway Oates of Bladen County, planter, for ₺ 30 proc. money, to Phillip Chavers of Craven County, South Carolina, planter, 100 A in Bladen County on little Pedee, granted to Robt Sweat, 23 Dec 1754...22 July 1772. Caroway Oates (Seal), Wit: Abram BArnes, Archd. McKissack. Nov Term 1774, Prov. by Abraham Barnes. Alfred Moore, Clk.

1738-1779

Pp. 425-426: N. C., Bladen County: John Branch of co afsd., planter, to Ł 30 proc. money, to Archd. Smith, planter, of same, land on Gum Swamp east of Drowning Creek, granted to Solomon Johnston, conveyed to John McCrary, by deed, by John McCraney, 22 Dec 1768, 100 A...below William Dreyers inprovement ...John Branch (Seal), Wit: Daniel Smith, Dannel Mcfallaw, Breton Branch. Nov. Term 1774, Prov. by Daniel Smith, Alfred Moore, Clk.

Pp. 426-427: 29 Oct 1774, Archd Little of Bladen co., to Neill Murfey of Cumberland Co., for Ł 15 proc. money, land in the prong of Dukemicars Branch, south of Rockfish Creek, near the head of a Spring Branch...150 A, granted to Archd. Little 22 May 1772...Archd. Little (Seal), Wit: John Legett, Malcolm Mcfall(?). Novr Term, prov. in court by John Legett. Alfred Moore, Clk.

Pp. 428-429: 6 May 1774, Abraham Hill of Hallifax Co., N. C., to Archibald Black of Cumberland Co., for Ł 20 proc. money...land in Bladen Co., about 3/4 mile above Solomon Johnstons survey, half a mile east of the Green Swamp, granted May 1773, 250 A...Abram Hill (Seal), Wit: James Gordon, John Hill. Novr Term 1774, prov. by James Gordon, Alfred Moore., Clk.

Pp. 429-430: 5 Jan 1774, Thomas Robeson of Bladen Co., NC, planter, for Ł 5 to Peter Robeson, land granted 17 Nov 1753, on NE side of NW River...Thomas Robeson (Seal), Wit: William Cain, Joseph Cain. Novr Term 1774, ack. in open court. Alfred Moore, Clk.

Pp. 430-431: 15 May 1774, Keneth Black of Cumberland Co., planter, to John Peterson, planter, for Ł 10 proc. money... land granted to Keneth Black 13 Oct 1760, on S side Rockfish Creek ...Keneth Black (Seal), Wit: James Marshall, John Legett, Novr Term 1774, prov. by John Legett. Alfred Moore, Clk.

Pp. 431-432: 25 March 1770, Joseph Fort of Bladen Co., planter, to Joseph Williams of same, cooper, for Ł 25...300 A purchased of our Soverign King George III 29 Sept 1756... Joseph Fort (Seal), Wit: Thomas Little, Tarler O Quin, Chembers Humphrey. Prov. by Thomas Little, Alfred Moore, Clk.

Pp. 432-433: 17 Oct 1774, William Toller of Bladen Co., to Peter McKeller, of same, for Ł 15 proc. money...land on S side Mill prong of the Raft Swamp, about a Mile above the Fork, 100 A...William Toler (Seal), Wit: John Legett, Murdoch McRa. Novr. Term 1774, prov. by John Legett. Alfred Moore, Clk.

Pp. 433-434: 3 Aug 1774, James Johnston of Bladen Co., to Thomas Little, planter, for Ł 20...land James Johnston purchased from Green Morgan in Bladen Co., on the Hill near Drowning Creek, granted 9 Jan 1772 & Goen Morgans patent, 28 Apr 1768...James Johnston (Seal), Wit: Stephen Andress, Robt Raiford. Ack. in court, Alfred Moore, Clk.

Pp. 434-435: 2 Aug 1774, James Johnston of Bladen Co., to Thomas Little of same, for Ł 25...100 A purchased from Jacob Pitman, adj. Oxendine, part of tract granted to Hector McNeill 6 May 1760, deed dated to James Johnston 14 July 1772...James Johnston (Seal), Wit: Stephen Andes, Robt Raiford. Ack. in Court. Alfred Moore, Clk.

1738-1779

Pp. 435-436: 16 Oct 1773, Henry Messar of Bladen Co., to Benjamin Britt, Blacksmith, of same, for Ł 12...100 A that the sd. Henry Messar purchased of George III 17 Dec 1769, above Jones's, Lord's...Henry Messer (Seal), Wit: Thomas Little, Tulla Daze. Prov. by Thomas Little, Alfred Moore, Clk.

Pp. 436-437: 5 Feb 1772, Thomas Mims & wife Grace of Bladen Co., to Thomas Amis, of Duplin co., for Ł 80 proc. money ...200 A surveyed by W Pugh the 20th day of Sept 1750 for Henry Sims, and by patent bearing dated 5 Apr 1753, conveyed to Thomas Mims...Thomas Mims (Seal), Grace Mims (Seal), Wit: Robert Sims, Jacob Likes. Feby Term 1772, prov. by Thos Mims & wife. Maturin Colvill, C. C.

Pp. 437-438: 27 Nov 1773, William Strickland Senr of Bladen Co., to Thomas Amis of same, for Ł 16 s 10 proc. money... 33 A, part of 150 A on Cubbages Swamp, granted to Gideon Klimum & by him conveyed Isaac Stevens, and by Stevens to William Strickland ...William Strickland Senr. (Seal), Wit: Dempsey Dawson, John Coleman, Phillip Stricklen. Prov. by John Coleman May Term 1774. Alfred Moore, Clk.

Pp. 438-439: 16 Jan 1773, John Butler of Bladen Co., to Thomas Amis, for Ł 80 proc. money...100 A on S side Drowning Creek, granted 5 May 1769 to John Butler...John Butler (Seal), Wit: James Brown, John Simpson, Restore Powell. Feby Court 1773, prov. by John Simpson. Maturin Colvill, C. C.

Pp. 439-440: ___ 1774, John Simpson of Bladen Co., to Thomas Amis of same, for Ł 24 proc. money...land on E side Drowning Creek, patent 12 May 1772...Jn. Simpson (Seal), Wit: Nicholas Irvin. Ack. May Term 1774. Alfred Moore, C. C.

Pp. 440-442: 13 July 1774, Joseph & John Price, planters, of Bladen co., to John McKay, planter of same, for Ł 80 proc. money...1/2 pd on this date, other 1/2 due White Sunday 1775, land on Bigg Marsh, 200 A...granted to the sd. Joseph and John Price, ___ Jan 1773...John Price (Seal), Joseph Price (Seal), Wit: Archd. McEacham, Murd__ Zaird (Laird?). Ack. in Court Nov. term 1774. Alfred Moore, Clk.

Pp. 442-443: Sylvanus Wilson of Cumberland Co., planter, for Ł 22 proc. money to Benjamin Atkinson of Bladen Co., planter, 200 A by patent dated 26 Nov 1757, granted to Daniel Chancy, sold to Silvanus Wilson, on Harrisons Creek...15 Apr 1774. Silvanus Wilson (Seal), Wit: Benjā. Cooepr, Saml Sutton. Ack. in court Nov. 1774. Alfred Moore, Clk.

Pp. 443-444: Joseph Oates of Craven Co., South Carolina, to Edmond Brown of Bladen Co., N. C., planter, for Ł 30 proc. money...100 A on a swamp called the Cowpen prong including Nicholas Princes improvement, a tract formerly granted to Joseph Oates, 19 Nov 1764...24 Sept 1771. Joseph Oates (Seal), Wit: Charles Barfeld, Thomas Brown. Novr Term 1774, prov. by Charles Barefield. Alfred Moore, Clk.

Pp. 444-445: N. C. Bladen Co.: James Johnston of co. afsd., for Ł 120 to John Cursey of same, planter, 200 A whereon the said James Johnston now lives, surveyed 3 Apr 1764 by Robt Edward, granted to Benjamin Odom, 2 Nov 1764, regr. Book 12, page 84... 9 Nov 1773. James Johnston (Seal), Wit: Abram Banus, Jacob

46

1738-1779

Caisey. Ack. May Term 1774. Alfred Moore, C. C.

Pp. 445-446: Nathaniel Sanders, for ₤ 5 proc. money to Hector
McNeill...land on W side Raft Swamp, granted to me
Dec 1768, 100 A...10 Dec 1773. Nathl Sanders (Seal), Wit: Antho.
Pouncy, Daniel Smith. Prov. by Daniel Smith. Alfred Moore, Clk.

Pp. 446-447: Benjamin Odom & wf Thamer, for ₤ 100 proc. money to
James Johnston...land whereon the said Johnston now
lives, 200 A, on S side Drowning Creek, surveyed 3 Apr 1764 by
Robert Edwards, granted to sd. Benja. Odom, 2 Nov 1764...10 Oct
1772. Benja. Odom (Seal), Thamar Odom (Seal), Wit: Archd McKissak,
William Moory. Prov. by Wm Moory, May Term 1774. Alfred Moore, CC.

Page 448: Thomas Odom of Bladen Co., for ₤ 100 proc. money to
John Smith, 150 A, SW of Drowning Creek about half a
mile above where it empties into the old field Swamp, granted
to Thomas Odom, 27 Apr 1767...18 Apr 1773. Thomas Odom (Seal),
Wit: Abraham Barnes, Josiah Barnes. Prov. by Abraham Barnes,
Alfred Moore, Clk.

Page 449: Benjamin Odom of Bladen Co., for ₤ 70 proc. money to
William Thompson, 100 A on S side Drowning Creek...3 Dec
1772. Benja. Odom (Seal), Tamer Odom (Seal), Wit: Abraham Barnes,
Michael Barnes. Prov. by Abram Odom. Alfred Moore, Clk.

Pp. 450-451: John Hadson of Craven Co., South Carolina for ₤ 55
proc. money, to John Starling of Bladen Co., land
on W side Drowning Creek, granted to Hector McNeill 25 March 1757,
conveyed to Stephen Cole, by deed 29 Oct 1757, thence to John
Hadson 10 Oct 1768...11 March 1772. John Hadson (X) (Seal), Wit:
Luke Pryor, William Coward. Novr Court 1772, prov. by William
Coward. Maturin Colville, C. C.

Pp. 451-452: N. C., Bladen County: John Grainger Junr, planter of
co. aforesaid, by my Bond executed 28 March 1764,
bound unto Richard Quince, Merchant, in Brunswick of the prov.
afsd., for ₤ 265 s 8 d 4 proc. money conditioned for the payment
of ₤ 632 s 10 d 8 proc. money, with interest ...also by bond to
Mr. John Quince...tract where I now live 640 A, adj. John Porter,
also negro slaves Jobe, Benny, Dinah, Kate, Comba, Benny, Jack,
Renty, Jeffrey, Jonny, Fibber, Peter, Diannah & Jemy...6 Oct 1772.
John Grainger Jr. (Seal), Wit: Samuel Neale, John Cheese. Prov.
by Samuel Neil, 18 Jan 1773. M. Moore.

Page 453: Alexander McDaniel of Bladen Co., planter, for ₤ 15 proc.
money, to Moses Tarliff of same, planter, 100 A on W
side of South River...Alexander McDaniel (A) (Seal), Wit: John
Edge, James West. May Court 1770, prov. by James West. Maturin
Colville, C. C.

Page 454: 4 Feb 1773, James Bailey of Bladen Co., merchant, to
William Moorehead, of same, planter, for ₤ 90 proc.
money..land bequeathed by Joseph & Eliphey Plumber to Jeremiah &
Joseph Plumber as pr Deed, 100 A...James Bailey (Seal), Wit: A.
McLaine, Maturin Colvill. Feby Court 1774, Ack. by James Bailey.
Maturin Colville, C. C.

Page 455: 9 Oct 1773, William Moorehead of co. of Bladen, to Peter
Byrne carpenter, of same, 1/2 of land bequeathed by

1738-1779

Joseph & Eliphe Plummer to Jeremiah & Joseph Plummer...William Moorehead (Seal), Wit: James Moorehead, Lowrence Byrne. Novr Term 1774, prov. by James Moorehead; Alfred Moore, Clk.

Pp. 456-458: 1 Oct 1771, Phillip Wood & wife Lucy of Bladen Co., to Thomas Robeson Junr of same, planter, for 87,000 feet of Merchantable lumber...land on NE side of the NW branch of the Cape Fear River, granted to Thomas Tenny, 28 Sept 1753, sold to Sampson Wood, 27 July 1759, and granted said 500 A to his son Phillip Wood by his last will & testament, 13 July 1759, adj. Phillip Wilkesons corner...Phillip Wood (Seal), Lucy Wood (X) (Seal), Wit: Ithamar Singletary, Peter Robison. Ack. by Phillip Wood & wife Lucy, 27 Feb 1772. M. Moore.

Pp. 458-460: 13 Nov 1773, William Morehead of Bladen Co., to Thos Robeson, for L 100 proc. money...land on upper side of Thomas Robesons land that he now lives on & on the lower side of land that John King now lives on, S side of the NW River of Cape Fear, 1/2 of 640 A patented by John Forster, 18 Nov 1760, confirmed to William Moorehead, Jean Moore Sarah Moorehead, 4 Nov 1761...William Moorehead (Seal), Wit: John King, Jas. Counsel. Prov. Feb. Term 1775, by James Counsel. Alfred Moore, C. C.

Pp. 460-461: N. C., Bladen County: 12 Aug 1774, O Quin Best of Edgecomb Co., N. C., planter, to Duncan Campbell of Bladen Co., for L 80 proc. money...200 A on W side Richland Swamp, adj. James Phares, granted to Jacob Pitman 27 Apr 1767...O Quin Best (Seal), Wit: Hugh Campbell, Daniel Campbell, Daniel Paterson. Feb. Term 1775, prov. by Hugh Campbell. Alfred Moore, C. C.

Pp. 461-462: N. C., Bladen County: 12 Aug 1774, O Quin Best of Edgecomb Co., planter to Duncan Campbell, planter, for L 50 proc. money...land on lower side of a tract granted to Jacob Pitman, sold to sd. O Quin Best on S side Richland Swamp, adj. Jacob Pitman, 200 A granted 25 Jan 1773...O Quin Best (Seal), Wit: Hugh Campbell, Daniel Paterson, Daniel Campbell. Feb Term 1775, prov. by Hugh Campbell. Alfred Moore, C. C.

Pp. 462-463: N. C.,Bladen Co.: Benjamin Odom for L 16 proc. money to Elizabeth Best of same, land on NE side of Drowning Creek about 8 or 9 miles above bear swamp, granted to Robert Edwards, 100 A, 9 Apr 1770, Reg. in Book 13, page 566... __ Sept 1773. Benjamin Odom (Seal), Wit: Richd Smith, John Carsey. Nov Term 1774, prov. by Richd Smith. Alfred Moore, Clk.

Pp. 463-464: 23 Jan 1775, Joseph Melton of Bladen Co., to Jacob Alfred, planter, for L 80 proc. money...100 A in N side Drowning Creek, part of 200 A granted to Hector McNeill, 6 May 1760 & also by a deed of conveyance from sd. McNeill to said Joseph Milton, 13 Sept 1764...Joseph Melton (Seal), Lusee Melton (3) (Seal), Wit: John Duman, Taler O Quint. Feby term 1775, prov. by Taler Oquint. Alfred Moore, Clk.

Pp. 464-465: 7 Sept 1773, Joseph Williams of Bladen Co., N. C., cooper, to Chambers Humphreys of same, for L 20... 100 A, part of a survey that Joseph Williams purchased of Joseph Fort, which Joseph Fort purchased of George III, 29 Sept 1756, on W side Saddle Tree swamp...Joseph Williams (Seal), Wit: Thos Littel, Mary Littel, William Littel. Prov. by Thomas Little, Alfred Moore, Clk.

1738-1779

Pp. 465-466: 29 Oct 1774, Joseph Williams of Bladen Co., planter, to John Hammon of same, for Ł 11, 100 A on Saddle Tree swamp, purchased of Peter Lewis, who purchased of George III, 8 Nov 1770, on Hollens or Willis upper line...Joseph Williams (Seal), Martha Williams (Seal), Wit: Thómas Little, Jesse Little. Prov. by Joseph Little. Alfred Moore, Clk.

Pp. 466-467: 2 Nov 1774, Solomon Messer of Bladen Co., NC, planter, land on Saddle Tree Swamp, 100 A, that sd. Solomon Messer purchased of George III 22 May 1772, near John Hammons upper line...Solomon Mercer (Seal), Wit: Jas. Smith, Saml Andros Junr. Ack. in open court, Novr. term 1774.

Page 467: 29 Oct 1773, Water Gibson, William Salter, James White James Bailey & Benjamin Humphrey, directors for the town of Elizabeth, to John Salter of Bladen Co...1/2 A lot in Elizabeth Town, #71...Wit: John White (S. M.), David Russ. Prov. by John White (S. M.) in court. Alfred Moore, Clk.

Page 468: 29 Oct 1773, Walter Gibson, William Salter, James White, James Bailey & Benjamin Humphrey, directors of the Town of Elizabeth, to James Salter, lot # 115...Wit: John White (S. M.) David Russ. Novr Term 1774, prov. by John White (S. M.). Alfred Moore, Clk.

Pp. 468-469: 18 Dec 1759, John Speir of Beaufort County, N. C., planter, to William Burney of Bladen Co., for Ł 200 proc. money, 360 A adj. Mr. Samuel Swan, on Wagamaw Lake, adj. Mr. Clayton, patented to Hon. Mathew Rowan, conveyed by him to Warren Baldwin and James Baldwin, 26 Feb 1741, and by Warren Baldwin to James Baldwin by deed, and by James Baldwin to Wm. Speir by deed 7 Apr 1752...John Speir (Seal), Wit: Hugh Pugh, Thomas Coomes. August Court 1760, prov. by Simon Burney. Jas. Burgwin, C. C. Reg. in Book E, fo. 111.

Page 470: William Burney of Bladen Co., N. C., for natural love & affection to my three children, Simon Burney, William Burney & Catrin Brocke, after my death, all household stouf (sic) & personal estate, goods, chattles and cattle, slaves (named) and 300 A...William Burney (LS), dated 1 Sept 1760. August Court 1770, ack. in open court. Wit: Rob Johnston, M. Moore. Maturin Colvill, C. C.

Pp. 471-472: 1 Dec 1774, William Horn & wife Jane of Bladen Co., to David Godwin of same, for Ł 60 proc. money... 160 A on S side Porters Swamp, on E side Drowning, where Wolfpit joins the upper side of John Yateses, to Oliver Stevens line, granted to William Horn 22 May 1772...William Horn (Seal), Jane Horn (Seal), Wit: Jon. Coleman, Coleman Nichols. Feby Term 1775, prov. by Coleman Nichols. Alfred Moore, Clk.

Page 472: 2 August 1774, Barnabas Stevens to David Godwin planters, for Ł 9 s 9 d 6 land on E side Drowning Creek near Smiths Bluff, 50 A...Barnabas Stevens (Seal), Wit: John Coleman, Coleman, Nichols. Prov. by John Coleman, Alfred Moore, Clk.

Pp. 473-474: 30 March 1773, Ignatius Flowers of N. C., Bladen Co., to Edward Grantham of same, for Ł 75 proc. money... tract below Timothy Obyans improvement, patent dated 29 Apr 1768, to Jethro Oates conveyed to sd. Flowers, 100 A on S side Ashpole

1738-1779

or Tadpole swamp, adj. Jethro Oates, Robert Edwards, and a patent 18 Nov 1771 to Ignatius Flowers...Ignatius Flowers (Seal), Wit: Thos Amis, Wm. Amis. Prov. by Thos Amis. Alfred Moore, Clk.

Pp. 474-475: 21 Dec 1774, William Horn & wife Jane of Bladen Co., to David Godwin of same, for ₤ 100 proc. money... land on S side of Cubbages Swamp of Drowning Creek, 250 A, part of 640 A granted to Gov. Tryon to John Willis...William Horn (Seal), Jane Horn (Seal), No wit. Prov. by Coleman Nichols, Nov term 1775. Alfred Moore, Clk.

Pp. 475-476: N. C., Bladen County: Abraham Barnes & Robert Edwards of co. afsd., to Josiah Barnes of same, for ₤ 60 proc. money...land on E side Ashpole or Tadpole Swamp, on the lower side of Horn Camp Branch or about ½ mile above the mouth thereof, 200 A granted 16 Dec 1769, to sd. Barnes & Edwards, Rec. in Book 14, page 531...1 Feb 1775. Abraham Barnes (Seal), Ro. Edwards (Seal), No wit. Ack. Feb. term 1775. Alfred Moore, Clk.

Pp. 476-477: 25 Dec 1773, Robert McRee of Bladen Co., to Richard Salter of same, for ₤ 130 proc. money...land on NE side of the NW River, 320 A, part of land taken up by Samuel Johnston Esqr, adj. Dennis Collums uper corner tree...Robert McRee, Jane McRee (Seal), Wit: William Salter, Thos Owens. May Term 1774, prov. by Thomas Owens. Alfred Moore, C. C.

Pp. 477-478: 23 Dec 1773, Benjamin Fitzrandolph to Robert McRee, the said Fitzrandolph being impowered by a power of attorney from Edmond Chancy for ₤ 50 s 5 proc. money, 320 A part of tract taken up by Samuel Johnston...Benja. Fitzrandolph (Seal), Wit: Elizabeth Fitzrandolph, Mary Fitzrandolph. Bladen May Term 1774, ack. in open court. Alfred Moore, C. C.

Pp. 478-479: 26 Apr 1775, Isaac Lamb of Bladen Co., to Robt Edwards of same, surveyor, for ₤ 50 proc. money... 200 A on Old Field Swamp...Isaac Lamb (Seal), Wit: Dan Willis, John Willis. May Term 1775, prov. by Danl Willis. Alfred Moore, Clk.

Pp. 479-480: Peter Simpson planter of Brunwsick Co., N. C. for ₤ 10 currency to Thomas Simpson of prov. afsd., planter...100 A on S side Bryans Swamp, a branch of Drowning Creek including his improvement and Indian old field, granted by Gov. Joseph Martin...31 Jan 1774. Peter Simpson (Seal), Hannah Simpson (Seal), Wit: William Bryan, James Simpson. Feb. Term 1775. Prov. by James Simpson. Alfred Moore, C. C.

Pp. 480-481: James Corbett of Brunswick Co., NC, planter, for love good will, to my loving daughter Ann Sellers wife of Matthew Sellers, 150 A, ½ of 300 A in Bladen Co., on the SW branch of Waggamaw below the White marsh, below Richland branch...5 May 1773. James Corbett (Seal), Wit: Arthur rollin, James Corbet, Simon Sellers, Ann Sellers. Ordered to be registered. Alfred Moore, Clk.

Pp. 481-482: N. C., Bladen County: Ann Perkins of co. afsd., for ₤ 20, to William Lowry, land on Beaver dam branch of Raft Swamp, which is a branch of Richland(?) Swamp, granted 2 May 1772, 100 A...Ann Perkin (X) (Seal), Wit: Thomas Powe, James Lowrey. Bladen May Term 1775, prov. by James Lowery. A. Moore, Clk.

50

1738-1779

Pp. 482-484: 14 Nov 1769, James White Esqr. high Sheriff of Bladen Co., to Joseph Kemp of same, cooper...by virtue of a writ from Superior Court for the Dist. of Wilmington holden May Term 1768...100 A belonging to John Huffman, on E side of Ashpole or Saddletree Swamp...sold to the highest Bidder 26 Nov 1768, for Ł 6 s 6 d 4...Jas White Sheriff (Seal), Ack. in open Court, May Court 1770. Maturin Colville, Cl.

Pp. 484-485: 28 Sept 1771, William Hall of Bladen Co., planter, to Enoch Hall of same, for Ł 30 proc. money...land on E side Drowning Creek adj. Gromes upper line, at present Lewis Halls line...William Hall (X) (Seal), Susannah Hall (ᘎ) (Seal), Wit: Lewis Hall, James Dulony. Prov. by Lewis Hall, Feby Court 1772. Maturin Colville, Cl.

Pp. 485-486: 25 July 1774, Enoch Hall of Bladen Co., to Lewis Hall Junr. of same, for Ł 30 proc. money...land on E side Drowning Creek about a mile below Lewis Hall Senr, 200 A ...Enoch Hall (Seal), Wit: William Beaty, Lewis Hall Senr. Prov. by Lewis Hall Senr; Alfred Moore, Clk.

Page 487: 28 Apr 1774, John Caisey of Bladen Co., planter, to Thomas Starlin of same, for Ł 25...land on E side Drowning Creek about three miles above the mouth of bear Swamp 150 A...John Caisey (Seal), Wit: Richd. Smith, Archd. McKissack. Ack. May Term 1774. Alfred Moore, Cl.

Pp. 488-489: 6 Jan 1775, John Smith Senr. of Bladen Co., planter, to Richard Grantham of same, planter, for Ł 12 proc money...land between Drowning Creek & Tadpole at a place called Turkey Island, granted to John Smith May 1772...John Smith (Seal), Wit: Thos Amis, Edward Grantham. Prov. by Thos Amis, Feb. Term 1775. Alfred Moore, Clk.

Pp. 489-490: 25 July 1774, Lewis Hall of Bladen Co., to Enoch Hall, for Ł 30 proc. money...land on E side Drowning Creek, adj. William Halls corner, granted May 1772...Lewis Hall (Seal), Wit: Lewis Hall Junr., John Legett. Ack. in court, Alfred Moore, Clk.

Pp. 490-491: 8 Apr 1768, James Inman & wife Elizabeth of Bladen Co., to Thomas Pitman of same, for Ł 25 proc. money ...land about three miles below Thomas Lambs plantation, granted 21 Oct 1758, 100 A...James Inman (Seal), Elizabeth Inman (Seal), Wit: Jesse Pitman, Isom Pitman. Bladen Novr. Court 177_, Prov. & Ordered to be registered. A. Howe, Cl co.

Pp. 491-492: 13 Apr 1775, William Hall of Duplin Co., planter, to Enoch Hall of Bladen Co., for Ł 20 proc money...100 A in Bladen or Anson on the Southwest side of Drowning Creek, just below overSheets old Bridge...William Hall (Seal), Wit: Lewis Hall, William Beaty. Bladen May Term 1775, prov. by Lewis Hall, Alfred Moore Clk.

Pp. 492-493: Archibald McKissak Esqr. of Bladen Co., for Ł 30 proc. money to John McCrainey of same, planter... land on SW side Ashpole swamp, about ¼ mile below the mouth of long branch, including the plantation James Doyall (Dogall?) formerly lived on, granted to sd. McKissak 15 Dec 1770...Archd. McKissak (Seal), Wit: Gilbert McCramey, John Turner. May Term 1775, Ack. in court, Alfred Moore, Clk.

51

1738-1779

Pp. 493-494: John Russ Senr, Planter of Bladen Co., for L 30 proc
money to William Russ of same, planter...land on W
side of the White Marsh, adj. William Hesters line...29 Apr 1775
John Russ (Seal), Wit: John Russ Junr. Prov. May Term 1775 by
John Russ Junr. A. Moore, Clk.

Pp. 494-495: 25 June 1774, Ann White, widow, Joseph White & Mary
White, son & daughter to the sd. Ann White, all of
Bladen Co., to John Dobbins & Lucy Young of Bladen Co., the
said Dobbins of the County of Cumberland and Lucy Young of Bladen
Co., for L 300 proc. money of N. C....1000 A granted to Richd
French (Trench?), on S side of the river, 7 Sept 1735...Ann White
(Seal), Joseph White (Seal), Mary White (Seal), Wit: J. Bowman,
John Brown. Bladen May Term 1775. Prov. by John Bowman, A.
Moore, Clk.

Pp. 496-497: 16 Nov 1770, John Cleborn of Bladen Co., Laborer,
to Daniel Willis of same, planter, for L 25 proc.
money...land on great Hogg Swamp East of Ashpole about a mile
above the fork of said Swamp, 150 A, the upper part of 300 A
patented by William Edwards & Conveyed to the sd. John Cleborn, 2
Augst last past, patent dated 16 Dec 1769...John Cleborn (Seal),
Wit: Joseph Bridges, George Willis. May Term 1775, Proved by
George Willis. A. Moore, Clk.

Pp. 497-498: N. C., Bladen County: Encoh Hall & Ann Hall, planter,
for L 17 s 15 proc. money to Alexander Graham, land
on N. E. Side Drowning Creek about a mile below Thomas Robison
Senr, granted 22 Jan 1773, 200 A...29 Apr 1775. Enoch Hall (Seal),
Ann Hall (Seal), Wit: John Gilchrist, Lewis Hall. May Term 1775,
proved by Lewis Hall. Alfred Moore, Clk.

Pp. 498-499: William Gray of Bladen Co., planter for L 30 proc.
money...to my cousin Andrew Graham, land on NE
River, 320 A...3 Octr 1758. Will Gray (Seal), Bladen County, Oct.
Court 1759. Prov. by James McDaniel.
Wit: John & James McDaniel. Registered in Bladen County, Book E
fo 97. John Burgwin, C. C.

Pp. 499-500: 15 Aug 1775, John Baxley of Bladen Co., to Robert
Upton, for L 45 proc. money...land on Ten Mile
Swamp, including teh plantation whereon John Baxley now lives
granted to Thomas Baxley 22 Apr 1763, and conveyed by deed to
John Baxley, 29 March 1765...John Baxley (Seal), Wit: John Legget,
Archd. McEacharn. Novr Term 1774, prov. by Arch.d McEacharn.
Alfred Moore, Clk.

Pp. 500-501: 18 Jan 1775, John Suister of Bladen Co., to William
Baxley of same, for L 20 proc. money...land on SW
side of the ten Mile Swamp, a little below John Baxleys land,
granted to John Suister 22 Dec 1770...John Scuister (Seal), Wit:
Thos Davis, John Baxley. Feb. Term 1775, ack. in court.
Alfred Moore, C. C.

Pp. 501-502: 20 Dec 1774, Ishmael Chavis & Reigel his wife of
Bladen Co., to Peter McArthur planter for L 40 proc.
money...100 A on lower side of long Swamp, NE of Drowning Creek
...Ishmael Chavins (X) (Seal), Reigel Chavis (X) (Seal), Wit:
Malcom Buie, John McArthur, Neill McArthur. Feby Term 1775,
prov. by Malcom Buie. Alfred Moore, Clk.

1738-1779

Pp. 502-503: James Pace & wife Mourning of Bladen Co., for Ł 50 proc. money to Malcom Buie of same, planter...200 A the upper part of 600 A granted to Henry Oberry 8 Oct 1748, and by deed from Oberry to Solomon Johnston, and by deed from Johnston to James Pace 10 Apr 1770, on the SW side of a Branch of Raft...23 Sept 1771. James Pace (Seal), Mourning Pace (Seal), Wit: Hugh Brown, Hugh McCraine. Prov. August Court 1772 by Hugh McCraine,;Maturin Colville, C. C.

Page 503: Thomas Cearsey made oath in open court this first Tuesday in Feby 1775 that he was an evidence to a Deed given by James Obery to Solomon Johnston for Two hundred acres of land being part of Six hundred & forty acres belonging to Henry Oberry the said Deed was dated in the year 1769 which Deed is lost. Thos Kersey. Taken in Court Feby term 1775. Alfred Moore, Clk.

Pp. 504-505: 8 Feb 1770, James White Esqr. late Sheriff of Bladen County, to William McRee of same, by writ of fi fa from the court for the Dist. of Wilmington, returnable 27 May 1771, to levy of the goods, etc. of Robert Johnston decd., Ł 1000 sterling...for Ł 15,100 A...Wit: Alexr Gray, David Linds. White. Feby term 1775, prov. by Alexr Gray. Alfred Moore, Clk.

Pp. 505-506: William McRee for Ł 25 proc. money to William Moore of Bladen Co., planter, land known as Johnstons Bluff...3 Aug 1775. William McRee (Seal), Wit: John King, James Moorehead. Ack. by McRee. A. Moore, Clk.

Pp. 506-507: Joseph Fort of Bladen Co., for Ł 10 proc. money, to John Gilchrist, planter of same...land on Mill prong of Raft Swamp, part of a survey of 300 A patented by Henry Obery 8 Oct 1748, & by his son James Obery to me conveyed, 70 A ...Joseph Fort (Seal), Wit: John McCraine, Joseph Regan. May term 1775, Ack. in court. A. Moore, Clk. Dated ____ 1770.

Pp. 507-508: 7 June 1774, Richard Bedghill of Bladen Co., planter, to Christopher Goodwin, for Ł 50 proc. money...100 A granted to sd. Richd. Bedghill Senr. by patent 22 Nov 1771... Richard Bedghill Senr (Seal), Wit: Luke Barefield, Richd Bedghill Junr. Novr. Term 1774, prov. by Richd Bedghill Junr. Alfred Moore, Clk.

Page 508: 7 Aug 1772, Archd. Shaw of Bladen co., Turner, to Archd. Taylor, Blacksmith of same, for Ł 25 proc. money... land on both sides Hammonds Creek adj. David Rouches survey & Neill Shaw, patent to sd. Archd. Shaw 22 Oct 1772...Archibald Shaw (Seal), Wit: Neill Shaw, Alexander Shaw. Novr. Term 1775. Prov. by Neill Shaw. Alfred Moore, Clk.

Pp. 509-510: 31 July 1775, Adam Ivey of Bladen Co., to John Sterling, planter, of same, for Ł 50 proc. money...land on Eastern edge of Ashpole or Tadpole Swamp, 200 A, granted 4 May 1769... Adam Ivey (X) (Seal), Wit: Daniel Willis, John Willis. August term 1775. Prov. by Danl. Willis. A. Moore, Clk.

Pp. 510-511: John Odom of Bladen Co., for Ł 20 proc. money to William Baker, 200 A granted to John Odom Dec. 1770 ...John Odom (Seal), dated 5 Sept 1771. Wit: Abram Barnes, Josiah Barnes. Feby Court 1772, prov. by Abram Barnes Esqr. Maturin Colville, C. C.

1738-1779

Pp. 511-512: 8 Feb 1775, Lewis Thomas of Bladen Co., farmer, to Cannon Cumbour of same, planter, land on E side of the great Swamp on the bottom of Gourleys Neck, adj. Thos Kinlows 100 A...Lewis Thomas (Seal), Wit: Stephen White, William Moore. (No prov. date)

Pp. 512-513: Abraham Strickland for ₺ 5 proc. money to John Duncan ...50 A on E of Drwoning Creek...26 July 1775. Abraham Strickland (Seal), Wit: Richd Smith, Alexander McLean. Bladen, August Term 1775, prov. by Richd Smith. A. Moore, Clk.

Pp. 513-514: 13 Apr 1774, Nathan Horn of Bladen Co., to James Rowland Senr., for ₺ 30 proc. money...land on play Hill branch east of Tadpole or Ashpole Swamp, adj. Daniel Willis, 200 A...Nathan Horn (Seal), Wit: Saml Smith, John Rowland. Prov. by Samuel Smith, May Term 1774. Alfred Moore, Cl.

Pp. 514-515: 31 Jan 1771, James Sanders of Craven County, South Carolina, to John Smith Senr. of Bladen Co., for ₺ 30 proc. money...land on E side Indian Swamp adj. 200 A possessed by a deed from Samuel Thornton to Stephen Cole, 340 A, part of 640 A granted to David Clark, and conveyed by him to Samuel Thornont, 340 A, from Thornton to sd. James Sanders 11 May 1764...James Sanders (Seal), Wit: Saml Smith, Wm _____. Prov. by Saml Smith, May Term 1774. Alfred Moore, C. C.

Pp. 515-516: 13 Apr 1774, Nathan Horn of Bladen Co., to John Smith Senr., of same, for ₺ 30 proc. money...land between Tadpole Swamp & Drowing (sic), adj. Murphys (sic)upper tract, 640 A...Nathan Horn (Seal), Wit: Saml Smith, John Rowland. Prov. by Samuel Smith, May Term 1774. Alfred Moore, Cl.

Pp. 516-517: 30 Apr 1774, Nathan Horn of Bladen Co., to John Smith Senr., for ₺ 30 proc. money...land on Flowers swamp between Tadpole and Drowning Creek, adj. Edward Flowers, James Blount...Nathan Horn (Seal), Wit: Saml Smith, John Rowland. May Term 1774, prov. by Saml Smith. Alfd. Moore.

Pp. 518-519: 6 March 1775, Isaac Lamb of Bladen Co., planter, to John Smith of same, planter, for ₺ 50 proc. money... 170 A, adj. Isaac Lamb, granted to Abraham Lamb 26 Nov 1757, conveyed to Abram Barnes by deed 28 Apr 1764, and from Abram Barnes to Isaac Lamb 1 Aug 1770...Isaac Lamb (Seal), Wit: Saml Smith, Danl Willis. August Term 1775, prov. by Saml Smith. A. Moore, Clk.

Pp. 519-520: Nathan Horn of Bladen Co., planter, for ₺ 16 proc. money, to John Smith Senr...land on W side Ashpole or Tadpole Swamp, below Chaves Thomsons lower line, 300 A, a tract granted to Charles Finkley, 16 Dec 1769...16 Jan 1775. Nathan Horn (Seal), Wit: Saml Smith, Susanna Smith. August Term 1775, prov. by Saml Smith. A. Moore, Clk.

Pp. 520-521: 6 March 1775, Isaac Lamb of Bladen Co., to John Smith of same, for ₺ 50 proc. money...land granted to Abram Lamb, 26 Nov 1757, conveyed by the said Abraham Lamb to Isaac Lamb 20 Oct 1758...Isaac Lamb (Seal), Wit: Saml Smith, Danl Willis. August Term 1775, Prov. by Saml Smith. A. Moore, Clk.

Pp. 521-522: 2 Aug 1775, Richard Smith of Bladen Co., to Nathaniel

1738-1779

Richardson of same, for Ł 20 proc. money...100 A on NE side Drowning Creek, a little below where Richard Smiths Bridge formerly Stood...Richd. Smith (Seal), Wit: Abraham Brown, Daniel Lind White. August Term 1775, Ack. by said Smith. A. Moore, Clk.

Pp. 523-524: 24 Dec 1774, Jacob Alfred of Bladen Co., planter to James McNeill of same., for Ł 180 proc. money...200 A on W side Gum Swamp, granted 29 Sept 1764, 100 A on W side of gum Swamp, east of Drowning Creek, granted to Jacob Alford, 4 Nov 1769, and 200 A....three tracts....Jacob Alford (Seal), Wit: John Legett, Archd. McEachern. Prov. by John Legett, Augst term 1775. A. Moore, Clk.

Pp. 524-525: 22 July 1775, James Stewart of Bladen Co., to John Slingsby of Wilmington, N. C., county of New Hanover, Merchant, for Ł 260 proc. money...292 A, part of 600 A granted to John Clayton 19 May 1736, for 584 A, and by said Clayton made over by indorsement on the Back of said patent 12 Aug 1736, to John DuBois, and by John DuBois, conveyed to John Jones, 31 Jan 1760, and by sd. John Jones & wife Ann, conveyed to Joseph Clarke 24 Sept 1764, by Joseph Clarke to sd. James Stewart 19 Dec 1766... James Stewart (Seal), Wit: William McNeill,John McNeill. August Term 1775, prov. by William McNeill. A. Moore, Clk.

Pp. 525-527: 10 July 1775, William Stewart & wife Jennet to William McNull (McNeill??), for Ł 300 proc. money... 540 A, part of 640 A granted to Gabriel Johnston Govr., 1738, to William Norton Senr., except one hundred acres adj. Richard Mallington, given to John Ingmore(?) by the last will and Testament of William Norton, 220 A of which was left to Thos Norton, and said Thomas Norton did by deed conveye to Daniel Norton, and sd. Daniel did by deed to sd. William Stewart, with 200 A of the said tract first mentioned which was left to Jacob Norton by the L. W. & T. of William Norton,conveyed by Jacob Norton to Daniel McNeill Esqr., and then to William Stewart...Wm Stewart (Seal), Jennet Stewart. Wit: Neill McCoulsby, David Bailey. August term 1775, Neill McCoulskey prov. A. Moore, Clk.

Pp. 527-528: N. C., Bladen County: James Duncan, planter, for Ł 18 proc. money, to Archd. Wilkeson, planter, land on NE side Drowning Creek, being a survey to me granted __ May 1773, 100 A...James Duncan. (Seal), Wit: John McNair, John Lordy. August Term 1775, prov. by John McNair. A. Moore, Clk.

Pp. 528-529: 15 Oct 1773, Walter Gibson, James Bailey, William Salter, James White & Benjamin Humphrey Trustees & Commrs. for the Town of Elizabeth in the County of Bladen, for s 40 proc. money to Joseph Dickson...½ A lot...Wit: John White, Joseph Humphrey. Bladen May Term 1775, prov. by Joseph Humphrey. A. Moore, Clk.

Page 529: Edward Flowers of Bladen Co., to John Barret, one parcel of cattle, and a parcel of Hogs (marks given)... 2 March 1775. Edward Flowers (Seal), Wit: Saml Smith, Drury Baret. Bladen, Aug. Term 1775. Prov. by Saml Smith. A. Moore, Clk.

Pp. 529-530: Edward Flowers of Bladen Co., to Drury Barret of same, lot of cattle & Hogs...2 March 1775. Edward Flowers (Seal), Wit: Saml Smith, John Barret. Prov. by Saml Smith, August term 1775. A. Moore, Clk.

55

Pp. 539-540: 30 Dec 1774, Hector McNeill of Bladen Co., to Neill McNeill of same, for Ł 60 proc. money...land on the western side of the Mill Branch of the Raft Swamp about five Miles above the Mouth, near Carvers lower line, 100 A...granted to sd. Hector McNeill 9 Apr 1770, the other tract on w side Mill prong 50 A... Hector McNeill (Seal), Wit: John Legett, Malcom Buie, Murd Macree. Feb. term 1775, prov. by John Legett. Alfred Moore, Clk.

Pp. 540-541: 28 Sept 1773, John McLaughlin of Bladen Co., to William Hester of same, for Ł 18 proc. money...land on SE side Nowles branch, adj. William Singletary, David Whites path, 80 A, granted to William McRee by Gov. Tryon, 16 Apr 1765... John McLaughlin (Seal), Wit: John Hill, David White. Prov. by David White. Alfred Moore, Clk.

Pp. 541-542: N. C., Bladen County: 30 Dec 1774, Thomas Johnston for Ł 150 proc. money...to John Wingate, 500 A on W side White Marsh...Thomas Johnston (Seal), Wit: John Drew, John Chicke, Deliah Drew. Prov. by oath of John Whingate. Alfred Moore, Clk.

Pp. 542-543: David Duncan of Balden Co., for Ł 50 proc. money to Thomas Dawson of same, Sadler...200 A granted to sd. David Duncan, 24 May 1773...6 Nov 1775. David Dunkin (Seal), Wit: John Wingate, John Wilson & Benja. Sellers. Ack. in open court. Alfred Moore., Clk.

Pp. 543-544: 4 Aug 1774, John Pemberton of Bladen Co., planter & wife Rebecca, to James Maultsby of same, planter, for Ł 32 proc. money...land granted to John Maultsby decd., conveyed to Edwd Pemberton, bequeathed to his son the said John Pemberton ...John Pemberton (Seal), Rebecca Pemberton (Seal), Wit; James Pemberton, Margaret Pemberton. Novr Term 1774, Ack. in court. Alfred Moore, Clk.

Pp. 544-545: 4 March 1775, Barnabas Stephen of Bladen Co., for Ł 50 proc. money to John Wingate of same, planter... land on W side White Marsh adj. William Hester, part of a tract of land patented for Thomas Hester 22 Nov 1758, 100 A...Barnabas Stevens (Seal), Wit: John Chicken, Arthur Robbins. Ack. in open Court. Alfred Moore., Clk.

Pp. 545-546: 29 Jan 1773, James Brown of Bladen Co., to Moses Coleman, for Ł 40 proc. money...land on S side of Cubbages Swamp of Drowning Creek, in the North corner of a tract patented by John Will taking in the plantation where Abraham Sapp formerly did live, 200 A...James Brown (Seal), Wit: Jno Simpson, Luke Barefield, Jno Coleman. Prov. Feb. Court 1773, by John coleman. Maturin Colville, C.C.

Pp. 546-547: 1 Oct 1774, Daniel Willis & Elizabeth his wife to Isham Pitman, of Halifax Co., Blacksmith, for Ł 20 proc. money...100 A patented to Daniel Willis May 1772...Daniel Willis (Seal), Betty Willis (Seal), Wit: Lott Pitman, Jesse Pitman. Alfred Moore, C. C.

Pp. 547-548: 3 Feb 1776, Lewis Muns of Bladen Co., to John Stewart of same, for Ł 170 proc. money...land on the upper side of Rockfish Creek, two tracts, including a Grist Mill & plantation, the patent by Henry Messer & conveyed to James Counsel, then to Alexr Gregory, then to John McMath, then to Phillip Ikner, then to Lewis Munse, 200 A...Lewis Munse (Seal), Wit: Murdoch McRae, James McNabb. Prov. by oath of Murdoch McRae. Alfred Moore, C. C.

Pp. 549-550: 1 Jan 1776, James Lewis of Bladen Co., planter to Josiah Lewis Junr. of same, for ₺ 50 proc. money.... land on W side of the Brown Marsh Swamp, land formerly surveyed for Jeremiah Bigford, 100 A, granted to Joseph Dixon by Gov. Tryon, 22 Dec 1770...James Lewis (Seal), Wit: Mathew Kally, James Shipman. Prov. by James Shipman. Alfred Moore, Clk.

Pp. 550-551: 2 March 1775, Thomas Dison & wife Martha of Bladen Co., to David Goodwin of same, for ₺ 30 proc. money ...land in the fork of Porters Swamp above Starkes plantation, 86 A...Thomas Dison (Seal), Martha Dison (Seal), Wit: Jon. Coleman, Nehemiah Johnson. Prov. by John Coleman. Alfred Moore, Clk.

Pp. 551-552: 13 Sept 1775, Coleman Nichols & wife Martha of Bladen Co., to Thomas Amis of same, for ₺ 10 proc. money... 38 A, part of 400 A granted to Joshua Smalley 22 Dec 1765, adj. Amis mill dam...Coleman Nichols (Seal), Martha Nichols (Seal), Wit: Josiah Lewis Junr, Elizabeth Hudson. Prov. by Josiah Davis. Alfred Moore, C.

Pp. 552-553: 3 Feb 1776, Silas Adkins of Bladen Co., to William Thomson of same, for ₺ 20 proc. money...land on Horse Swamp east of Ashpole or Tadpole Swamp, granted to Thomas Odom 16 Dec 1769, conveyed to Silas Adkins 10 Dec 1774...Silas Adkins (Seal), Wit: Abraham Barnes, Archd. McKisak. Prov. by Archd. McKissak. Alfred Moore, Cl.

Pp. 553-554: 2 March 1772, Joseph Dickson of Duplan (sic) Co., N. C. Yeoman, to James Lewis of Bladen Co., planter, for ₺ 15 proc. money...land on W side Brown Marsh Swamp, formerly surveyed for Jeremiah Bigford...Joseph Dickson (Seal), Wit: Robert Koron, James Shipman, William Stevens. Prov. by James Shipman, May Court 1772. Maturin Colvill, C. C.

Pp. 554-555: John Burgwin of Wilmington, Merchant, bound to David Godwin in the sum of ₺ 200 proc. money...15 June 1774, land on Drowning Creek adj. John Wilson Senr plantation where he now resides, 640 A, conveyed by patent to John Stark formerly of said county, Schoolmaster, conveyed to sd. John Burgwin by deed about 1760....Jno Burgwin (Seal), Wit: Frans. Child. Prov. by Frances Chil. Alfred Moore, Cl.

Pp. 555-556: 22 Apr 1774, Berroni Clayton of Bladen Co., to John Roberts, for ₺ 24 proc. money...land on the NE side of Cape Fear River on the S side of NW branch, 150 A....formerly belonged to John Clay...Benoni Clayton (Seal), Wit: Thos Owen, Is. Wood. Prov. by Thos Owen, Alfred Moore, Clk.

Pp. 556-557: 13 Aug 1774, John Dunn Senr of Anson County, Blacksmith, & wife Mary to Joseph Cooper of Bladen Co., for ₺ 280 proc. money...land on W side of the NW River adj the lower line of Sarah Westfield, granted to Richard Dunn, 13 Sept 1735, 320 A, conveyed to John Dunn...John Dunn (Seal), Mary Dunn (Seal), Wit: Benja. Cooper, John Dunn, Jesse Codail. Prov. by Benja. Cooper. Alfred Moore, Cl.

1738-1779

Pp. 558-559: 13 Aug 1774, John Dunn Senr. of Anson Co., & wife
            Mary, Black Smith, to Joseph Cooper, for ₤ 100
proc. money...land adj. 160 A, adj. Daniel Shipman, Richard Dunn,
granted to Sarah Lewis, 13 Sept 1735...John Dunn (Seal), Mary
Dunn (Seal), Wit: Benja. Cooper, John Dunn, Jesse Doccil. Prov.
by Benja. Cooper, A. Moore, Clk.

END OF VOLUME

1791-1804

N. B. This volume begins with page 407.

Page 407: __ and Fifty Acres in Bladen Co., on East side of Gapeway Swamp...pr patent dated 20 Dec 1792

State of N. C. No. 1715, for L 50 specie for every 100 A, granted to Anguish Shaw 150 A in Bladen Co., on S side of Cow branch...pr patent dated 20 Dec 1791

State of N. C. No. 1727, granted to Daniel Shipman, 33 A in Bladen Co., on E side of the white marsh, adj. Greens corner, pr. patent dated 20 Dec 1791

No. 1823 State of N. C. Josiah Singletary, 150 A in Bladen Co., East of the Great Swamp adj. John Harrison, pr patent 20 Dec 1791

State of N.C. Nov. 1677, grant to John Smith, 100 A in Bladen Co. on west side Jannegess (?) Bay, Bogue Swamp, patent __ Dec 1791

Page 408:
State of N. C. No. 1762, grant to Simon Smith, 50 A on the Big branch of the Beaver Dam Swamp, patent 20 Dec 1791

State of N. C. No. 1819, grant to John McDaniel, 100 A East of Great Marsh, patent 20 Dec 1791

State of N. C. No. 1868, grant to Neill McNorton (McNoughton) 97 A on the N side of the Brown Marsh, near Charles McNaughton ...patent 20 Dec 1791

State of N. C., No . 1815, grant to John King, 200 A on the grate Swamp including a white oake Island, 20 Dec 1791

Page 409:
State of N. C. No. 1806,grant to Matthew Kelley, 100 A on west side of the Brown Marsh, 20 Dec 1791

State of N. C. Nov. 1766, grant to John McKay, 100 A on S side Horse shoe swamp, near"Babtist hole" , 20 Dec 1791

State of N. C. No. 1825 grant to Archd. McDaniel, 200 A south of South River including the head of Watsons branch, near his own line...20 Dec 1791

State of N. C. No. 1730, grant to Alexander Graham, tract on Wild Horse neck (acreage not given), near McCalpins line, 20 Dec 1791

Page 410:
State of N. C. No. 1744, grant to Jas. Isham, 50 A on higgins Meadow spring, about ten yards from the Springs, 20 Dec 1791

State of N. C., No. 1696, grant to Benjamin Woodard, 100 A on both sides Slapass Swamp, 20 Dec 1791

State of N. C., No. 1878, grant to Jacob Guyton, 100 A adj. Jacob Guytons old line, on the Beauford swamp, 20 Dec 1791

State of N. C. No. 1856, grant to John Green, 50 A on SW side of the watry branch, 20 Dec 1791

1791-1804

Page 411: State of N. C. No. 1672, grant to Charles Edwards 100 A on E side of Burnies ___(?), patent 20 Dec 1791

State of N. C., Nov. 1832, grant to Elizabeth Evans, 200 A near the plantation whereon she now lives, near Jeremiah Willis line patent 20 Dec 1791

State of N. C. No. 1897, grant to Jared Ervin 50 A on the lower side of Ervins land, patented by Solomon Spiars, and on the upper side of Jourdan's land, patent 20 Dec 1791

State of N. C. No. 1741, grant to Henvy Colvill, 100 A on boggy branch, patent 20 Dec 1791

State of N. C., Nov. 1873, grant to Richd. Collum, 100 A south of pine log swamp, near the head, patent 20 Dec 1791

Page 412: State of N. C. No. 1731, grant to George Clark, 100 A on E side of the old Horse Swamp, adj. Thos Johnson patent dated 20 Dec 1791

State of N. C. No. 1712, grant to Moses Coleman, 100 A on horns mill swamp, adj. horns land and Ames land, adj. William Stevens corner, patent 20 Dec 1791

State of N. C, Nov. 1829, grant to Moses Coleman 150 A on south side of Syprus branch, adj. John Colemans, 20 Dec 1791

State of N. C. No. 1820, grant to Moses Holmes, 200 A on NW River, on the south side of a branch of White creek, 20 Dec 1791

Page 413: State of N. C., No. 1740, grant to Nathan Horn, 50 A on S side of Ashpole, 20 Dec 1791

State of N. C. No. 1681, grant to Elisha Herell, on NE of Saddle Tree, 20 Dec 1791

State of N. C. No. 1777, grant to Nathan Horn, 100 A on SW side of the great Cowpen swamp, adj. his own line, 20 Dec 1791

State of N. C. No. 1781, grant to William Parker, 50 A on E side of the Richland branch, adj. William parkers corner, 20 Dec, 1791

State of N. C. No. 1760, grant to Joseph Baldwin, 50 A on the East of the white marsh, adj. Robt Greens(?) corner, 20 Dec 1791

Page 414: State of N. C., grant to Henry Boswell, on the North side of Morleys branch, adj. Sessions corner, his own corner, 20 Dec 1791  No. 1724

State of N. C. No. 1728, grant to William Boswell, 100 A in the fork of Madams branch, adj. Hardicks line, 20 Dec 1791

State of N. C. No. 1718, grant to Nathaniel Baldwin, 50 A on the east side of the white marsh on Cherry tree branch, adj. Robt Greens, John Faulks corner, 20 Dec 1791

State of N. C. No. 1723, grant to Edward Wilson, 100 A on the Beaver Dam swamp, 20 Dec 1791

1791-1804

Page 415: State of N. C. No. 1894, grant to Lewis Williamson, 100 A on N side of Dun swamp, and west side of Horse swamp, 20 Dec 1791

State of N. C. No. 1733, grant to Elias Fiveash, 100 A on W side Wilkisons swamp, 20 Dec 1791

State of N. C., No. 1824, grant to Elias Fiveash, 200 A on W side Wilkisons swamp, 20 Dec 1791

State of N. C., No. 1767, grant to William Parker, 100 A on E side of peocoson Branch...near great Swamp, 20 Dec 1791

Page 416: State of N. C. No. 1782, grant to Coleman Nickels, 100 A on W side of Porters swamp, adj. William Horns, wolf trap branch. 20 Dec 1791

State of N. C, No. 1755, grant to Stephen Fester, 200 A on S side of Turnbull. 20 Dec 1791

State of N. C. No. 1764, grant to Richard Lewis, 100 A on E side Bryans Swamp, 20 Dec 1791

State of N. C. No. 1751, grant to John Davis, 100 A on E side of Turnbull Creek, adj. Russ, Sallars, 20 Dec 1791

Page 417: State of N. C. No. 1884, grant to Thos Ard, 100 A on E of Drownding Creek near or joining Charles Clamdine line, 20 Dec 1791

State of N. C, No. 1893, grant to Joshua Lee, 100 A in the fork of Horsepen branch and grate swamp, adj. Lennon, 20 Dec 1791

State of N. C. No. 1790, grant to John Lennon, 293 A on NE side of NW River, granted 20 Dec 1791

State of N. C. No. 1679, 50 A on S side Ceader branch, granted 20 Dec 1791, grant to Jethro Robbins.

Page 418: State of N. C. No. 1842, grant to John Russ Junr., 110 A on N side Bryans Swamp, adj. Ridings, 20 Dec 1791

State of N. C., No. 1743, grant to Thos Fitzgearreld, 200 A on N side of the Brown Marsh swamp, adj. Sarah Groves, 20 Dec 1791

State of N. C. No. 1881, grant to Thos FitzGerrald, 50 A on N side of the Brown Marsh swamp

State of N. C. No. 1710, grant to Wm Sibbit, 50 A on SE side of Cor branch, 20 Dec 1791

Page 419: State of N. C. No. 1780, grant to Caleb Granham, 50 A on Brown Marsh swamp, adj. Green, Baldwin, 20 Dec 1791

State of N. C., No. 1811, grant to Absolom Powell, 100 A on both sides of the western prong, 20 Dec 1791

State of N. C. No. 1870, grant to William Boice, 50 A on N side Dunns Swamp, adj. James Nelson, 20 Dec 1791

1791-1804

State of N. C. No. 1686, grant to Micajah Hill, 100 A on S side Duns swamp, adj. John Duns line, 20 Dec 1791

Page 420: State of N. C. No. 1883, grant to Josiah Davis, 100 A on both sides Little Cowpen swamp, 20 Dec 1791

State of N. C, No. 1674, grant to Benjamin Moor, 720 A on the great Swamp on Reggans path adj. Thos Peter and John Robeson, beginning at Peter Robeson, adj. Thos line, including the marsh 20 Dec 1791

State of N. C. No. 1690, grant to Arthur Braswell, 100 A on S side of Ashpole or Radpole, 20 Dec 1791

Page 421: State of N. C. No. 1662, grant to Thos Brown, 300 A on SW side of the Northwest branch of Capefear River adj. William Bembow, Swendles corner, 20 Dec 1791

State of N. C. No. 1826, grant to Robert Raford, 100 A on the head of the Beaver Dam Bays adj. Kelleys line, 20 Dec 1791

State of N. C. No. 1784, grant to Edward Jones, 150 A on Brery(?) branch, 20 Dec 1791

State of N. C. No. 1737, grant to William Jones, 88 Acres on SW side of the NW branch of Cape Fear River, adj. land formerly Ephraim Vernans (Vernons), 20 Dec 1791
Page 422:
State of N. C. No. 1828, grant to Lucey(?) Smith, 100 A on N side of Cape Fear River, adj. Dowlans corner, 20 Dec 1791

State of N. C. No. 1841, grant to John Sinklar, 50 A on both side of Cott(?) Branch, 20 Dec 1791

State of N. C. No. 1713, grant to William Summersett, 100 A on S side of Gapway swamp, 20 Dec 1791

Page 423: State of N. C. No. 1721, grant to Thos Simpson Junr, 150 A on both sides Bryans swamp, adj. John Russ Junr, Thos Bryan, 20 Dec 1791

State of N. C. No. 1778, grant to Stephen Hester, 50 A on NE of Crawley swamp, 20 Dec 1791

State of N. C. No. 1846, grant to Thos Richardson, 100 A on Bogue branch, 20 Dec 1791

Page 424: 17 March 1792, Leonard Dyson of Bladen Co., to William Boswell of same, for L 30 specie.:.100 A on Johnsons swamp...Leonard Dyson (Seal), Wit: Daniel Burney, Thomas Brite, Bladen Feby 1793. Provl by Daniel Burney. J. Singletary, C. C.

Pp. 424-425: N. C. Bladen County: In 1789 judgement was had before Thos Owen Esqr. by Robt McRee against Jared Ervin for the sum of L 20 specie, directed to Robt. Baker then Constable commanding to levy of the goods, etc. of Jared Ervin... land known by the name of Crowsons old place adj. near Bartrams Lake, near Waltar(?) Gibsons, 300 A which land after executed by the constable made his return in May 1790, then directed to John Ellis Shff...William McRee became the highest bidder for his father Robert McRee, for L 1 s 1 specie...29 Aug 1791. John

1791-1804

Ellis Shff (Seal), Wit: Wm Andres, Evan Ellis. Bladen Feby term 1793, prov. by William Anders, J. Singletary, C. C.

Page 425: William Jas Watson of Bladen Co., do sell to Capt. George Thomas a certain negrow wench Ana and her three children Anny, Lydia Minder and Lerinah...9 Nov 1792. Wm. Jas Watson (Seal), Wit; J. Ellis, J. Randolph Singletary. Feby term 1793,prov. by John Ellis.

Page 426: Recd. of Bradley and Cowan, Ł 230 for two Negrow slaves Peter and Gilbert, late property of John Grange Senr Decd. Gilbert fell to me by Division and Peter by consent of John Grange Junr...5 July 1788. Thos Neale Junr. Bladen Feby Term 1792. Prov. by James Purdre(?).

For Ł 500 pd. by Robt Scott, 16 negroes (named)...3 Sept 1792. Ralph Miller (Seal), Wit: Thos Scott, Benona Clayton. Bladen Feby Term 1793. Ack. in open court

John P. Grange of Brunswick Co., N. C. for Ł 135 to William Sallar Senr. of Bladen Co., N. C., negro wench Alice...16 June 1792. John P. Grange (Seal), Wit; Donald Bana. Prov. Bladen Feby Term 1793.

Page 427: Bladen Co., William Jones for Ł 120 to Joseph Richard Gotier, negro named Young Jim bought by me at a vandue of certain effects of the Late John Wen decest. Feb. 27, in the XII year of American independence. Wm. Jones (Seal), Wit: Daniel Bane. Prov. Feby Term 1793 by Daniel Bain.

Bladen Co., John McKay for Ł 40 pd. by Bradley & Cowan, negro Jim 8 Nov 1792. John McKay (Seal), Wit: James White, John Yates. Prov. by Jas. White, Feby Term 1793.

Page 428: 6 March 1792, John Husk Esqr. of Wilmington and Jas. Hogg surviving Exrs. of Robt Hogg, about the 10th of July 1786, at the sale of the goods and chattles, etc. of Christofer Gooding, late of Bladen by Jas. Purdie Sheriff, the said John Huske being the highest bidder for five several messuages and tract of land, all in Bladen Co., Ref. being had to the said deed registered in Book D pages 415 415 416 417 418 July 25th 1787..sold to Archd Buie two of these tracts that called the Indian place and that called McAlpins place and also sold to John Stewart another of three tracts called McPhailes place...now for s5 to James Hogg....John Huske (Seal), Wit: Donald Bain. Prov. by Bain Feby term 1793.

Pp. 428-429: N. C. Bladen County; whereas at a County Court of P & QS held for the county afsd., on the 8th of Nov. 1792, a judgement was had against John McKenne(?) for the sum of Ł 7 s 2, and execution passed 1 Dec 1792 directed to the sheriff of the county, to levy of the goods, etc. of the said John McKinne...Saml Richardson, Sheriff, do sell, 450 A on NE side of Drownding Creek joining fear Bluff plantation, the Creek Swamp, three tracts of land formerly possessed by Thos Amis...sold to Return Strong, the highest bidder...5 Feb 1793. S. Richardson Shff (Seal), Wit: J. McRee. Bladen Feby Term 1793, ack. in open court. J. Singletary C. C.

N. B. An error in pagination occurs here: the page following 429 is 450.

64

1791-1804

Pp. 429-450: 12 Jan 1793, Richard Faulk of Bladen Co., to William Stevans of same, for Ł 20 specie...100 A, part of a tract of 640 A granted to Thos Amis, and sold by him to John McKimrie, and from him to sd. Richd. Faulk, near Wolf pitt... Richd. Fault (Seal), Wit: John Hinnant, Jonathan Faulk (+). Feby Term 1793. Ack. in open court.

Pp. 450-451: 4 Feb 1793, Benjamin Eason of Bladen Co., to Return Strong of same, for Ł 100 specie..land on both sides of Gapway swamp, above the mill, 100 A patented by Benjamin Eason...the mark of Benjamin Eason (Seal), Wit: W. Bryan, N. Richardson. Bladen Feby Term 1793, Ack. in open Court, and ordered be registered.

Pp. 451-452: N. C. Bladen Co., whereas at a county court held in County of Wayn on the second monday in Jan. 1782, a judgment was had agaisnt Simon Fault for the sum of 40,000 pounds value to Ł 50 specie...to levy of goods, etc. of Simon Faulk Ł 50 specie, tract of 640 A, which James Holaman became the highest bidder, and admited the Rite and Title of sd. land to be made of Richd. Fault of Bladen Co...S. Richardson Shff (Seal) dated 27 Dec 1791. Wit: Amis Richardson, Jas. Hollamon. Bladen Feby Term. 1793, prov. by Amis Richardson. J. Singletary, C. C.

Page 453: N. C., Bladen County: Wm. Ellis, James Smith, Stephen Ellis, Elenor Ellis of county afsd., for Ł 100 current money sell unto Enoch Herrin, negrow wench Rose about 17 or 18 years of age...5 Feby 1793. Wm. Ellis (Seal), James Smith (Seal), Wit: M. Byrne, Stephen Andres. Feby Term 1793, ack. in open court.

Joseph Richd. Gautier admr. of the goods, etc. which were of George Win late of Brunswick Co., decd., to Ereck (Eneck?) Laconstadt of Bladen Co., Esquire, three negrows, (named), and amounts specified for each, 10 March 1792. J. R. Gautier. Wit: John Lewis Tayler, Jno Hall. Feby Term 1793, ack. in open court.

Page 454: Joseph Richd. Gautier admr. of Geo Win decd., for Ł 140 slave Dembo, to Saml Beall Richardson...10 March 1792. J. R. Gautier (Seal), Wit: Edward Jones. Bladen Feby Term 1793. Ack. in open court.

Recd. of Bradley & Cowan Ł 120 for negrow boy called Jim. 26 March 1792. Wm. Williams (Seal), Wit: C. A. Beloat. Suck Williams(?). Bladen Feby Term 1793, prov. by C. A. Beloat.

Page    : Powell Benbow do oblige myself at the Instance and Request of the said Wallar(?) Morgan, to make titles ...8 June 1759. Powell Benbow (X) (Seal), Elis. Benbow (E) (Seal), Wit: Wm. Bartram, John Leweas. Ack. 8 June 1759. Jas. Hasell, J (This appears to be a part of another volume, and the first portion of the preceding instrument missing. The next page bearing pagination is numbered 460).

Page    : Jas West of prov. of N. C., Bladen Co., planter, for Ł 10 proc. money, pd. by John Cashwell of same, planter ...land on West side of South River, 100 A...27 Apr 1770. James West (Seal), Wit: Jacob Sikes, John Baker. May Term 1770, ack. in open court. Maturin Colvill, C. C.

1791-1804

Page     : David Lloyd to Geo Thomas, 17 A on S side of Little
          Colley swamp, part of survey patend. by Waltar Gibson,
and sold by sd. Gibson to David Lloyd...(date missing) David Loyd
(Seal), Ann Loyd (Seal), Wit: John Garven, Jno Smith.  Feby
Term 1793. Ack. in open court.

Page 460: 4 Feb 1793, Thamon Singletary of Bladen Co., to Phillip
          Hill of same, for Ł 20 specie...100 A on both sides of
the Reedy branch...Thamore Singletary (Seal), Wit: Jo Singletary,
Snowden Singletary.  Feby term 1793, ack. in open court.

Pp. 460-461: 5 Feb 1793, John McKay of N. C., Bladen Co., to
          Colin Connerly of the other part, for Ł 60...50 A
adj. Crawfords line, above McKay rice field...John McKay (Seal),
Wit: Bartram Robison, Wm Ward.  Bladen Feby term 1793, prov.
by William Ward. J. Singletary, C. C.

Pp. 461-462: 3 Sept 1792, Ralph Miller, Esqr. of Bladen Co., to
          Robt. Scott, for Ł 500 current money...land on SW
side of the NW branch of Cape fear River, by grant 436 A, adj.
Jas. Dowey, John Waddell, also 200 A on Horse Shoe Swamp...
Ralph Miller (Seal), Wit: Thos Scott, Benoni Clayton.  Bladen
Feby term 1793. Ack. in open Court. J. Singletary, C. C.

Pp. 462-463: 5 Apr 1792, William Register of Bladen Co., to Cade
          Weatherly of same, for Ł 80 specie, 100 A between
Werrell branch and the big swamp...William Register (X) (Seal),
Wit: John Shaw, Jas. McKoulikey.  Feby Term 1793, ack. in open
court.

Pp. 463-464: 22 Jan 1793, William Gray of Bladen Co., to William
          Bedsole of same, for Ł 15...50 A between Turnbull
and the pine pond...William Grey (Seal), Wit: Hezekiah Jones (X),
Saml Hales (X).  Bladen, Feby Term 1793, prov. by Hezekiah Jones.

Pp. 465-466: Eleazer Russ carptr. Jas Russ, Joseph Russ, all of
          Bladen Co., to Thos Russ of same, planter, for Ł
100, 370 A patented by John Russ decd. in 1770, adj. John Singletary...Eleazer Russ (X), JAmes Russ, Joseph Russ (Seal), Wit:
John Singletary, Thos Mulford, John Garven.  Feby term 1793,
prov. by John Singletary.

Page 466: Rcd. February 4th 1793 of Hugh Murphy Ł 120 NC money
          negrow girl Fanny...Wm. Penett(?) (Seal), Wit: George
Thomas, John Smith.  Prov. by Geo Thomas, Feby term 1793.

Pp. 466-467: 19 Oct 1780, Joshua Lee to Arthur Chesnut, for Ł 30
          100 A on E side Drowning Creek...Joshua Lee (Seal),
Wit: Joshua Lee Junr, Stephen Lee.  Prov. Feby Term 1793, by
Stephen Lee.

Page 467: 20 Jan 1793, Wm. Stevens of Bladen Co., planter, to
          Benjamin Werrell of same, for Ł 50 specie...250 A
on W side White Marsh, adj. line now possessed by John Faulk,
Sarah McNichols...William Stevans (Seal), Wit: Eli Stevans, Michael King.  Bladen Feby 1793, ack. in open court.

Pp. 468-469: 29 Sept 1792, Wm. Fokes to Josiah Fokes, for Ł 50
          proc. money...97 A on SW side of the White Marsh...
William Fokes (Seal), Wit: John Fokes, Thos Sanders.  Ack. in
open court, Feby 1793.

1791-1804

Page 469: John Cockrell for 200 Silver dollras pd by Coleman Nickles of Bladen Co., negrow woman Annis...20 Oct 1792. John Cockrell (Seal), Wit: Simon Godwin, Ephraim Nickles. Feby term 1793, prov. by Simon Godwin.

State of N. C. No. 1791, grant to Joseph Kemp, 32 A in Johnsons lake, 20 Dec 1791

State of N. C. No. 1894, grant to John Kemp, 100 A on panther branch, 20 Dec 1791

Page 470( fragmentary): Powell Benbow and wife Elizabeth for ₤ 20 proc. money to Waltar Morgan...land on Carvers Creek adj. Garson Benbow, granted 5 Feb 1754, 350 A, conveyed by Saml Pike to Powell Bembow 4 March 1757...(end of this deed appears to be on page of this volume following page 454--see p. 65 of this book.)

END OF VOLUME

N. B. The remaining fragment of this volume begins on page 93.

Page 93: (first part of instrument missing): adj. Wm Hesters corner...to John Hester. J. Spiller (Seal), Wit: Lewis Barge Junr, Wm. Cook. Prov. by Wm. Cook and ordered to be registered June Term 1804. J. S. Purdie, C. C.

Pp. 93-94: Joshua Johnston of Bladen Co., to my son Enoch Johnston, my right claim & title to a certain sorrel mare about 4 years old (described), household furniture...4 June 1804 Joshua Johnson (Seal), Wit: Jacob Johnson, Saml Johnson.

Pp. 94-95: N. C., Bladen County: whereas at a County Court of CP & QS held for the county afsd. on Monday in ___ a Judgment was had by Philip Ward against Wm Ellis for ₤ 37... 100 A, piece of a tract purchased by Cornelious Pernell of Solomon Lewis...Jesse Jones by his attorney or agent James Jones became the last and highest bidder at the sum of ₤ 16... J. Lewis Shff (Seal), Wit: James Mears, Jona. Mears. Ack. June Court 1804. J. S. Purdie, C. C.

Pp. 95-96: Joshua Johnson of Bladen Co., to my son Wm. Johnson land in Bladen Co., between the Lake Bay and Harrison Creek Swamp, adj. Saml Carmon, granted by patent to Margaret Johnston, 640 A, 17 Sept 1773, also one tract adj. the same, 28 A granted to Hardy Valentine 17 Oct 1800, also one other tract on Harrisons Creek adj. James Johnson, known by the name of Woods Cabin, 390 A, patent to James Johnson 29 Sept 1779...4 June 1804. Joshua Johnson (Seal), Wit: Saml Johnson, Jacob Johnson. Prov. by Jacob Johnson, June Term 1804. J. S. Purdie, C. C.

Pp. 96-98: 5 March 1803, Baley Sutton of Sampson Co., N. C. to Joshua Johnson of Duplin Co., for 600 silver dollars ...land between the Lake Bay and Harrison Creek Swamp, 640 A granted to Margaret Johnson 17 Sept 1794, and other tracts (same land as in preceding deed.)...Baley Sutton (Seal), Wit: Jno Hufham, Jacob Johnston. Prov. by Jacob Johnson, June Term 1804.

1791-1804

Pp. 98-99: 5 June 1804, John Sutton of Bladen Co., planter, to Joel Johnston of same, for L 200 specie...land No. of the Juniper branch adj. Wm. Saltars corner, 200 A granted to John Sutton,by patent 13 Aug 1802...John Sutton (Seal), Wit: Francis Meekes, Christopher Sutton. Prov. by Francis Meekes. June term 1804. J. S. Purdie, C. C.

Page 99: N. C. Bladen County: Danl. McAllister appoint friend Jas. Kelly my true and lawful attorney, to collect money due me...23 Oct 1799. Danl Macallister. (Seal), Wit: John MacMillan, M. Philips. Prov. by Mark Philips. J. S. Purdie.

Pp. 99-100: N. C. Bladen County: Isaac Sullivan for 320 Dollars Federal money to Angus Lemon, planter...Isaac Sullivan, now of same county, late of Northampton County...negro girl Melinda 12 years old...13 Feb 1804. Isaac Sullivan (Seal), Wit: J. R. Gauture. Prov. by J. R. Gautier, June term 1804. J. S. Purdie, C. C.

Pp. 100-101: 8 March 1804, Frederick Simpson of New Hanover Co., N. C., to Archd. McKay of Bladen Co., for L 52... 53 A on NW branch of Cape Fear River in Bladen Co., adj. John Singletarys corner, nearly opposite to the mouth of Hammons Creek...Fredk. Simpson (Seal), Wit: Daniel Campbell, J. McKay. Prov. by Danl Campbell, J. S. Purdie. C. c.

Pp. 101-102: 3 March 1803, Danl Campbell Senr. of Bladen Co., to Major John McKay & Sanl Campbell Junr, for 20 dollars N. C. currency...land between Upton and the double branch adj. Blue, McKeithan, McViters(?), Clarks, Maulsbys, Sims, McKays, Campbells, & McLousa & Ballentines 300 A, adj. corner of 150 A survey where Dugald Clark now lives.-.Danl. Campbell (Seal), Wit: Archd. Campbell. Prov by Archd. Campbell, June Term 1804. J. S. Purdie.

Page 102: State of N. C. No. 2406, grant to Joseph R. Gaurier, 150 A on E side of the White Marsh Swamp on both sides of Brick Kiln branch. Entered 7 Feb 1792. Patent dated 2 Oct 1801

Pp. 102-103: State of N. C. No. 2763, grant to James Currie, 170 A entered 23 Apr 1803. patent dated 30 Aug 1803.

Page 103: Joseph Kemp Senr for love good will and affection to my granddaughter Anne Jane Poynter, lot in the town of Elizabeth, 1/2 A No. 32...22 Feb 1803. Joseph Kemp (Seal), Wit: J. Ellis, Mary Poynter. Prov. March Term 1803 by J. Ellis. J. S. Purdie, C. C.

State of N. C. No. 2769, grant to Mathew Kelly, 200 A on the Brown Marsh Swamp, adj. Bigfords line, entered 13 Nov 1800. Patent dated 13 Oct 1803.

Page 104: N. C. No. 16. George III to John Simpson, 200 A on the E side Drowning Creek adj. Joseph Pates 50 A survey. Patent dated 14 May 1772.

N. C. No. 144, George III to Joshua Stephens 100 A on E side Drowning Creek adj. Joseph Oates, Butler, patent dated 18 Nov 1771.

1791-1804

Pp. 104-105: State of N. C. No. 2260, grant to Thomas Nicholas
Gautier, 400 A on the back of Fair Bluff, adj.
James Syniths line, patent dated 6 Dec 1799.

Page 105: No Carolina No. 519, George III to Joseph Oats, 50 A
adj. Thomas Mims, 27 April 1767

State of N. C., No. 1070, grant to John McKinne, 500 A
on W side Drowning Creek adj. Thomas Amis, patent dated 7 Aug
1781.

Pp. 105-106: 20 Feb 1777, Joshua Stevens of Bladen Co., to Thomas
Amis of same, for Ł 102 proc. money...150 A granted
to Joseph Oats by patent 27 Apr 1767, and by him conveyed to
Joshua Stevens...100 A granted to sd. Stevens 18 Nov 1771...
Joshua Stevens (Seal), Wit: Lewis Taylor, Wm. Waide, Marma.
Rawles. Prov. in June Court by Lewis Taylor. John White, C. C.

Page 107: 28 Oct 1778, Patrick Story of Bladen Co., to Thomas
Amis, for Ł 50...land on E side Drowning Creek, 200
A Patrick Story (Seal), Wit: John Yates, Josiah Barnes. Prov
by John Yates. John White, C. C.

Pp. 107-108: 6 Nov 1783, Thos Hayne Esqr. & wife Eliza to Jared
Ervin Capt. all of Bladen Co., N. C., for Ł 300
specie...1/2 lot in Eliza. town where the said Thos Haynes lately
lived...Thos Haynes (Seal), Wit: Isaac Jones, Wm. McKee. Bladen
Novr term 1783, ack. in open Court. J. White, C. C.

Page 108: State of N. C. No. 1011, grant to John Roberts, 640 A
on both sides Craisly Swamp, dated 25 July 1774.

Pp. 108-109: 3 May 1768, Joseph Oats of Bladen Co., to Joshua
Stevens of same, for Ł 20 proc. money...land on E
side of Drowning Creek, adj. Thomas Mims, on S side Cubbage
Swamp...Joseph Oats. (Seal), Wit: Peng(?) Johnson, Isaac Stevens.
Bladen Court 1768, ack. by Joseph Oats. A. Haw, C. C.

Page 110: State of N. C. No. 602, grant to Jacob Hanchey, 200 A
on E side Drowning Creek, patent dated 4 March 1774.

Pp. 110-111: 26 May 1804, Bailey Sutton to James Meredith, both
of Bladen Co., for 100 dollars...200 A on S side
South River adj. Beaman Sutton, Merediths lines. Bailey Sutton
(Seal), Wit: John Meredith. Ack. by Bailey Sutton, June Term
1804. J. S. Purdie, C. C.

Page 111: 9 Dec 1800, John Meredith, Elizabeth Meredith, Hannah
Meredith, William Haw Meredith, James Meredith,
Joseph Meredith, Ellinnor Meredith and Jane Meredith of Bladen
Co., to Nathan Meredith, for Ł 100...all that tract of land which
is aloted to our Mother Elizabeth Meredith as her dower during her
natural life, and at her deceased the said John Elizabeth Hannah
William Haw James Joseph Elennor and Jane being the true and
lawful heirs...Wit: Alexr Kelsoe, Sam Anders. Prov.by Alexander
Kelsoe, June Term 1804. J. S. Purdie.

Pp. 111-112: Duncan Stewart and James Stewart both of Montgomery
Co., Tennessee, do appoint Hugh Murphy of Bladen
Co., NC, our lawful attorney, to convey all land ..22 Feb 1804.
D. Stewart (Seal), James Stewart (Seal), Wit: James Bailey,

69

1791-1804

Jesse Deusone. Prov. by James Bailey, June Term 1804. J. S. Prudie, C. C.

Pp. 112- : N. C. 24 May 1803, Benjamin Smith of Beloadin(?) in
Brunswick planter, to Thomas Owens of Bladen Co.,
planter, for 300 dollars...land on NW branch of Cape Fear River
adj. plantation of Thomas Owens, known by the name of Finney Begue,
320 A which formerly belonged to Nathaniel Rice Esq. and lately
to Jacob Leonard deceased and was by deed from the heirs of
Jacob Leonard conveyed to sd. Benjamin Smith...(remainder of
deed missing.

N. B. Pp. 113-116 are missing.

Page 117: ...Thompsons corner, Brights line, entered 6th Feb 1800
patent dated 9 Nov 1803.

State of N. C. No. 2791, grant to John McEwen 300 A on Thompsons line, Millicans corner, William Hendersons line, entered 7 Nov 1801. Patent dated 9 Nov 1803.

Pp. 117-118: State of N. C. No. 2823, grant to Daniel Melvin, 50
A adj. Jonathan Thomas, entered 9 Nov 1796. Patent
dated 10 Dec 1803

Page 118: State of N. C. No. 2837, grant to John Melvin, 50 A
on N side Peters Creek, adj. James Moorehead, John
Cashwells line, entered Nov. 23, 1802, Patent dated 16 Dec 1803.

State of N. C. No. 2854, grants to John Sellars 100 and 40 acres
on E side Colly Swamp. (no date)

State of N. C. No. 2342, grant to James Smith, 100 A near the
Harrisons Lake, No of the head of the Buck Branch, Entered
13 Sept 1796. Patent dated 15 August 1800.

Page 119: State of N. C. No. 2230, grant to Beaman Sutton, 108 A
on S side of South River, adj. William Sutton, entered
5 May 1788. Pattent dated 7 June 1799.

State of N. C. No. 2805, grant to Edward Simpson, 150 A on the
road that leads from Elizabeth to Drownding Creek, Entered 12 May
1801, Pattent dated 29 Nov 1803.

State of N. C. No. 2667, 50 A on both sides of Bold Branch,
to Lazarus Turner, adj. Daniel Turner decd., William Hendersons
line, entered 22 March 1800, pattent dated 23 Nov 1802.

Page 120: State of N. C., No. 2828, grant to William Smith, 50 A
on SW side South River adj. John Smith, about 50 yards
west of the Wilmington Main Road, Entered 2 March 1801. Patent
dated 10 Dec 1803.

State of N. C. No. 2311, grant to Luke White, 150 A ½ mile
below the house where George White formerly lived, adj. Cornelius
Strawhorn, entered 17 May 1791. Patent dated 15 Aug 1800.

Pp. 120-121: State of N. C. No. 2895, grant to Richard M. Lewis,
near the head of Simpsons branch, enetered 5 Jan 1803,
Pattent dated 18 Oct 1804.

1791-1804

Page 121: State of N. C. No. 2793, grant to William McEwen, 100 A adj. Brights line, entered 6 Feb 1800, Patent dated 9 Nov 1803.

State of N. C. No. 2750, grant to Elias McGee, 100 A on Lucas Neck, adj. James Smith, James Cain, entered 9 Jan 1802, patent dated 11 Aug 1803.

Pp. 121-122: State of N. C. No. 2751, grant to Elias McGee, 50 A in Lucas Neck, adj. Jacob Smith, on N side Ellis Creek, entered 9 Jan 1802, dated 11 Aug 1803.

Page 122: State of N. C. No. 2589, grant to William White, 50 A within the lines of 200 A survey pattented by Isaac Jones deceased now said Whites, on E side Turnbull Swamp...entered 1 Oct 1800, patent 13 Aug 1802.

State of N. C. No. 2590, grant to William White, 100 A on E side Jones Creek, adj. Saltars, entered 16 Nov 1798, patent dated 13 Aug 1802

Pp. 122-123: State of N. C. No. 2591, grant to William White, 50 A on E side Turnbull Swamp adj. William Stewart Whites corner, on NE side Whites Mill branch, entered 1 Oct 1800, patent dated 13 Aug 1802.

Page 123: State of N. C. No. 2803, grant to Hugh Murphy, 340 A, near Waddels corner, entered 22 July 1803, patent dated 26 Nov 1803.

State of N. C. No. 2787, grant to Hugh Murphy, 100 A on S side Cypress Creek adj. Lloyds corner, McNabbs, Stephen Smith, entered 1 June 1802, patent dated 21 Oct 1803.

Pp. 123-124: State of N. C. 2785, Hugh Murphy, 230 A adj. his own corner, adj. Suttons line, Waddels, entered 1 Jan 1803, pattent dated 21 Oct 1803

Page 124: State of N. C. No. 2804, Hugh Murphy, 290 A adj. Walter Gibsons, Waddles line, entered 22 July 1803, patent dated 26 Nov 1803

State of N. C. No. 2175, Joseph Singletary, 100 A on the head of Whites branch, adj. Widow Simpsons corner, entered 25 Apr 1798, pattent dated 9 March 1799.

Page 125: John McKay of Bladen Co., for 450 spanish milled dollars to Argulas Poynter of same, negro Sam known by the name of Cooper Sam...4 June 1804. J. McKay (Seal), Wit: William R. Dunham. Prov. by W. R. Dunham, June Term 1804. J. S. Purdie, S. C.

Pp. 125-126: John & Joseph Plummer & John Lansdell all of Bladen Co., to James Saml Purdie, all of the land chattels real and things in action that were of the late Zachariah Plumer formerly of the County of Bladen now deceased... 179 . John Plummer (Seal), Joseph Plummer (Seal), John Lansdell (Seal), Wit: Masgrove Jones, Wm. McKee. Prov. by Musgrove Jones, J. S. Purdie, C. C.

71

1791-1804

Pp. 126-127: 10 Apr 1804, Abraham Blackwell of Bladen Co., to Edward Reaves of same, for ₺ 20 proc. money...land on W side Turnbull Swamp, 100 A. Abraham Blackwell (X) (Seal), Nancy Blackwell (Seal), Wit: Benjamin Davis, William Reaves. Prov by Benjamin Davis, June Term 1803. J. S. Purdie, C. C.

Pp. 127-128: 5 Sept 1803, Michel Thomas of Bladen Co., to Jonathan Thomas of same, for ₺ 100...a certain tract excepting the use of me Michel Thomas & Jane my wife...200 A...Michel Thomas (X) (Seal), Wit: Henry Thomas, Isam Weathersby. Prov. by Henry Thomas June Term 1804. J. S. Purdie, C. C.

Pp. 128-129: 12 Jan 1804, Moses Parker of Bladen Co., to Jorden Williford of same, for ₺ 100...2 tracts (1) land adj. George Brown, part lost by an older survey entered by Dennis Lennon near an old tar Kill, 95 A (2) land on N side Bain Swamp adj. Moore Lennons line, Parkers corner...Moses Parker (Seal), Wit: George Lennon, Moore Lennon. Prov. by Moore Lennon, June Term 1804. J. S. Purdie, C. C.

Pp. 129-130: 8 Sept 1803, T. W. Harvey of Bladen Co., planter, to Mathew R. White of Elizabethtown citizen, for ₺ 150...lot #49 in Elizabethtown...TW Harvey (Seal), Wit: D. W. Kemp, J Lewis.

Page 130: M. R. White for ₺ 150 to Gautier and Richardson, the aforementioned lot...15 Sept 1803. M. R. White, Wit: A. M. Hooper. Prov. by A. M. Hooper, June Term 1804.

Pp. 130-131: N. C., Bladen Co., Uriah Flowers for $100 to Laban Williamson, planter, for 150 A of land adj. Bright on Panther branch...August 1803. Uriah Flowers (Seal), Wit: Stephen Godwin, Louis Williamson. Prov. by <u>Richard</u> Williamson, June Term 1804. J. S. Purdie, C. C.

Page 131: State of N. C. No. 2794, grant to John Sutton, 640 A near Duncan Rays land, entered 24 Apr 1801, patent dated 10 Nov 1803.

State of N. C. No. 2797, grant to Willis West, 150 A on Rays Branch, adj. Stewarts line, entered 7 Apr 1793, pattent dated 23 Nov 1803.

Pp. 131-132: State of N. C. New Hanover County, Robert Murphy, planter, for ₺ 25 NC currency, to Burrel Blackbourn of Sampson Co., planter...land adj. John Treadwell, 300 A... 22 Dec 1802. Robert Murphy (Seal), Wit: H. Blackbourn. Prov. by H. Blackbourn, Sept. Term 1804, J. S. Purdie, C. C.

Pp. 132-133: 1 June 1804, John Curry of Bladen Co., N. C., planter, to Duncan Curry of same, for ₺ 25...land on both sides of the watering hole branch, on N side Rayburns bay, 100 A...John Curry (Seal), Wit: J. Kelly, Mary Kelly (X). Prov. by J. Kelly, Septr term 1804. J. S. Purdie, Clk.

Pp. 133-134: Daniel Schaw of Bladen Co., for $200 to Thomas Chancey, negro girl Nell...3 May 1804. Schaw (Seal), Wit: John McNaughton, Alexr McFatter. Ack. in open Court, Sept. term 1804. J. S. Purdie, Clk.

Page 134: John Clark of Isle of White County, Virginia, for $175 to John Chancey of Bladen Co., N. C., negro girl Vitel...9 Dec 1802. John Clark (Seal), Wit: Isaac Powel, Brittain Hargrove. Prov. by Brittain Hargrove, Sept. 1804. J. S. Purdie, C. C.

Pp. 134-135: 15 Aug 1804, Richard Holms to John Clark, both of Bladen Co., for $200...100 A pattented by the afsd. John Clark Senr dated 11 Nov 1779, also tract of 100 A pattented by John Turner dated 16 Dec 1769, conveyed by Clark to Hargrove 28 Aug 1776, conveyed to Wm. Wilkerson April 1786, then to sd. John Clark Senr 7 Apr 1798, 100 A granted to Britain Hargroves, 23 Oct 1782, conveyed to William Wilkeson 10 Apr 1786, then to John Clark Senr 7 Apr 1798, and by Clark to sd. Holms 25 Aug 1800...Richard Holms (Seal), Wit: Gabrel Holms. Ack. in open Court, Sept 1804. J. S. Purdie, C. C.

Page 136: 3 Sept 1804, Elisha Morpe of Bladen Co., to Dugal Ray of same, whereas Elisha Morpe Esqr. former Sheriff did execute a certain parcel of land on Whites Creek by grant 200 A the property of Duncan McCordsby(?) decd for the public tax... purchased by Hugh Waddle Esqr. for ₤ 20, laid out for Duncan McCoulsky 16 Dec 1752, granted 19 May 1753 by Mathew Rowan Pres. of N. C. &c...Elisha Morpe Sheriff (Seal), Wit: Richard Holms. Ack. in open Court. J. S. Purdie, C. C.

Pp. 136-138: 1 May 1804, Amos Johnston of Duplin Co., NC, to Robert Dowey and Daniel McKay both of same, land on S side NW River including the head of Carvers Creek, adj. Samuel Pike, Sal. Swindell, John Gray Blount, Frances Parker, by Watering Hole branch, includes 200 A to Danl Barnard and 100 A to Isaiah Sike, total 1850 A ...A Johnston (Seal), Wit: Jesse Johnston, Benjamin Elwett. Prov. by Benjn. Elwell, Sept 1804. J. S. Purdie.

Page 138: Jonathan Singletary of Bladen Co., planter, son of Mary Singletary, for ₤ 100 to Samuel Elkings the younger of same, planter, land on E side Crawley Swamp on S side Singletarys Swamp, 270 A, conveyed unto me by my uncle Benjn. FitzRandolph under the denomination of his loving cousin by deed 19 Oct 1784... 27 July 1804. Jonathan Singletary (Seal), Wit: Daniel Gooden, John Kelly Junr, W. R. Dunham. Prov. by Daniel Gooden, Sept term 1804. J. S. Purdie.

END OF VOLUME

Adair, James 10, 39
Adams,      1, 38
Adare, John 31
  Joyce 31
Adear, John 12
Adkins, Aaron 13
  Silas 58
Alford, Jacob 3, 11, 55
Alfred, Jacob 48, 55
Allen,      32
Amis, Thomas 1, 46(2), 50, 51,
             58, 64, 65, 69(2)
  Wm. 50
Anders, Sam 69
  Samuel 43
  Stephen 56
  William 64
Anderson, John 17
  Joseph 17
  William 36
Andres, Stephen 65
  William 64
Andress, Stephen 45
Andrews, Aba 43
  John 17
  Samuel, 43
  Stephen 17
Andros, Samuel Jr. 49
Arbee, Samuel 20
Ard, Thomas 36, 62
Aslae, Saml. 20
Atkins, Silas 17
Atkinson, Benjamin 46

Babon, Thomas 20
Bagget, Jesse 3
Baggot, James 24
Baggott, Shadrick 13
Bailey, David 55
  James 1, 3(3), 18, 20, 21,
         38, 43, 47, 49, 55, 56,
         69, 70
Bain, Daniel 64
  Donald 64
Baines, Abram 16
Balden, James
Baldwin, James Jr. 8
  James Sr. 8, 49
  John 44
  Joseph 61
  Nathaniel 61
  Warren 49
Baley (see Bailey), James 2
Ballard, John 38
Baker, John 65
  Robert 63
  Samuel 26(2)
Baba, Donald 64
Bane, Daniel 64
Banon, Joseph 43
Banus, Abram 46
Barefeett, William 31
Barefeld, Charles 46
  Joshua 5
  Luke 53, 57
  Mary 5
  Precilah 25
  Richard 5, 29, 32, 33
  Roger 25
  William 25
Baret, Drury 55
Barfield, Stephen
Barge, Lewis 67
Barlow, Willm 30
Barnard, Danl 73
Barnes, Abraham 4, 9, 11, 13(2),
                 44, 47, 50, 58
  Abram 13, 16, 44, 53
  Josiah 11, 47, 50, 53, 69
  Michael 47
Barret, Arick 56
  John 55, 56

Barrot, William 6
Bartram, William 12, 27, 30,
                   35(3), 65
Bartrom, Willm. 4, 29
Bartrum, William 26
Bas(?), Moses 34
Baswell, Henry 3
Baughart, John 14
Baxley, Edmund 43
  John 52
  William 52
Beard, James 17, 44
  John 4, 8, 12, 19, 28, 44
  Neill 4(2), 5
Bearfield, Rodger 6, 25
Beasly, Benjamin 44
Beaty, Bridgell 22
  William 51
Bedghill, Richard 53
  Richard Jr. 53
Bedsole, Wm. 66
Begford, Jeremiah 38
  Magdaleen 38
Beggs, James 37
Belnnard(?), Samuel 5
Beloat, C. A. 65
Bembow, William 63
Benbow, Charles 6
  Elizabeth 65, 67
  Garson 67
  Gershom 6
  Powell 65, 67
Bennett (Pennett?), Wm. 66
Berry, Robert 5
Best, Elizabeth 48
  O'Quin 48
Bigford, Jeremiah 16, 58(2)
Beggs, James 37
Bird, Henry 17
  Thomas 29
Black, Archibald 36, 37, 44, 45
  Keneth 45
Blackbourn, Burrel 72
  H. 72
Blackwell, Abraham 72
  Nancy 72
Blount, James 6, 27, 28, 29
  John 3, 28, 36, 43, 44
  John Gray 73
  Martha 28
  Philip 3
  Sarah 28
Blue, Mary 41
  Neill 41
Blunt, James
Boath, John 44
Boice, William 62
Boone, James 27, 34
Boswell, Elizabeth 1
  Henry 2, 61
  William 61, 53
Bottis, Francis 42, 43
Bound, Anne 15
  James 15
  James Jr. 15
  Jesse 15
  John 15, 23
  Mary 15
Bounds, Jesse 23
Bowdey, Jno. 25, 26
Bowman, John 52
Boyd, Jane 4
  John 3, 4
  Richard 43
Bracewell, David 32
  Richard 32, 56
Bradie, Alexander 1
Brady, Owen 24
Branch, Beslon 37
  Breton 45
  John 37, 45
Branche, John 36

Braswell, Arthur 63
Brawlevy, Joshua 22
Brett (Britt?), Benja. 37
Brewer, John 8
Brice, Malcom 32(2), 39
Bridges, James 13
  Joseph 52
Bright, Simon 44
Brite, Thomas 63
Britt, Benjamin 37, 46
  Lamb 14
  Nathan 15
Britton, Joseph 27, 30
  Stephen 27, 30
Broades, Peter 29, 34
Brock, Catrin 49
  Stephen 29
Brompton(?),    13
Browder, Thomas 1, 6, 16
Browdey, Jno. 25, 26
Brown, Edmund 46
  George 8, 14, 16, 24, 35, 43,
         72
  Hugh 22, 23, 33(3), 39, 53
  James 18, 40, 46, 57
  John 18, 26(2), 29, 34, 35, 52
  Mary 26
  Neil 33, 39
  Thomas 8, 32, 46, 63
  T. 42
Bryan, Jane 23
  John 23, 44
  Philemon 28, 44
  Thomas 63
  W. 65
  William 38, 50
Budbedg, John 26
Buffking, Benjamin 19
Buie, Archibald 64
  Francis 1
  Malcom 40, 52, 57
Bull, Francis 2
Bulley, Mathew 44
Burgeson, Elais 24
Burgwin, Jas. 49
  J. 27, 38, 40
  John 2(2), 3, 7, 9, 17, 21, 22,
        25, 33, 35, 42, 52, 58
  Margaret 2
Burney, Daniel 63
  Simon 49
  William 49
Burrough, Jones 28
Busbe, Nathaniel 43
Busby, Benjamin 20
Butler, John 46
  Joseph 43
  Samuel 34, 44
  Thomas 31
Byme(?), Lawrence 8
Byrne, Lawrence 39, 48
  M. 65
  Mathew 21, 39
  Peter 22, 39, 47

Cade, Elizabeth Hobson 38
  John 38, 39
  Jno. 15, 38
Cain, James 71
  Joseph 45
  Samuel 19, 20
  William 25, 26, 45
Caisey, Jacob 47
  John 51
Cameron, James 20
  John 20
  John Jr. 21
  Mary 20, 21
Campbell, Archibald 42, 68
  Capt. 38
  Daniel 48, 68(2)
  Donald 41

Duncan 48
Farquard 30
Hugh 42, 43, 48
James 16, 40
John 4, 43
Saml. 68
Canady, Solomon 16
Caraway, Thomas 33
Carman, Samuel 34, 67
Carmon, Saml. 67
Carpenter, Benjamin 27
Carsey(?), John 9, 31, 48
Carver, Betsy 32
Isom 32, 56
James 31, 39, 43
Jesse 31
John 31
Robert 32, 56
Saml. 31, 34
Sampson 31
William 3, 29, 32
Cashwell, John 65, 70
Cearsey, Thomas 53
Chambers, Bridget 24
William 24, 26(2)
Chancey, Daniel 17, 18, 46
Edmond 4, 50
John 73
Thomas 72
Chandler, John 7
Chapman, Alexander 13, 30
Chase, Anna 14
Chavers, Phillip 44
Chaves, Philip 11
Chavins, Ishmael 52
Chavis, Ishmael 52
Reigel 52
Cheaten, Richard 4
Cheese, John 47
Chessen, Richard 4
Chestnut, Arthur 66
Cheves, Philip 11
Sele 11
Chicke (Chicken), John 57
Chil. Tan. 42
Child. Frances 58
Zans 43
Claudine, Charles 62
Clardy, James 42
Clark, Benjamin 48
David 1, 15
Dugald 68
George 61
James 25
John 43, 73(2)
Joseph 15, 18
Clarke, Benjamin 39
Joseph 33, 34, 38, 55
Clay, John 58
Clayton, Benona 64
Benoni 58, 66
Berroni 58
Jno. 2, 8, 25, 26, 33, 35, 55
? 13, 49
Zebulon, 32, 52
Clerborn, John 52
Clemmond, William 38
Clibam, John 12
Cliborn, John 12
Clitherall, John 4
Clyburn, John 13
Cochran, Robert 2
Cockrell, John 67
Codail, Jesse 58
Cole, Alice 15, 23
James 29
John 13, 15
Mack 15
Mark 23
Stephen 15, 47
Coleman, Jno. 57
John 40, 46, 49, 57, 58, 61
Jon. 49, 58
Moses 40, 57, 61

Nichols 40
Phebe 40
Collins, Dennis 33
Rosum(?)12
Collom, Dinish 21
Collson, Chester 18
Collum, Richard 61
Collums, Dennis 50
Colman, John 1
Colsol, Chester 18
Colvill (Colville, Colill?),
(Martin, Maturin)
4, 5, 6, 7, 8, 9, 10,
11, 12, 13, 14, 15, 16,
17, 18, 19, 20, 21, 22,
23, 24, 25, 26, 27, 28,
29, 30, 31, 32, 33, 34,
35, 36, 40, 42, 44, 46,
47, 49, 51, 53, 56, 57,
58, 65
Henry 61
Comer, Widow 38
Conaway, John 18
Conner, Elender 42
Connelly, John 42
Connerly, Colin 66
Consey, Thomas 39
Coolper, Binja. 46
Cook, Wm. 67
Coomes, Thomas 49
Cooper, Benjamin 7, 18, 23(2),
36(3), 58, 59
Isaac 4, 17, 18
Jesse 7, 6
Joseph 6, 7(3), 10, 17, 18, 23,
36, 37, 58, 59
Mary 7, 10, 18, 23, 36
Prodence 17
Corbett, Abel 5
Brinkley 5
James 50
Council, Arthur 3
Counsel, James 48, 57, 58
Coward, William 47
Crawford, John 15
Creel, Lazarus 10, 43
Thomas 41
Cumbour, Cannon 54
Currie, James 68
Curry, Duncan 72
John 43, 72
Cursey, John 46

Dallison, John 35
Danns, 34
Darrah, Arched. 1
David, Francis 43
John 27
Davis, Able 43
Benjamin 9, 10, 72
Edward 20, 26, 44
Jno. 30
John 35, 42, 62
Josiah 58, 63
Richard 8
Thomas 4, 33, 37, 41, 43, 52
William 43
Dawson, Dempsy 1, 40, 46
Thomas 57
Day, Bunbury 22
Daze, Tulla 46
Deare, Jonathan 34
Dentry, Benja. 20
Deusone, Jesse 70
Dickson, Joseph 55, 58
Dionery, Robert 5
Dison, Martha 58
Thomas 58
Dixon, Joseph 58
Dobbins, John 52
Dobbs, Arthur 4, 23
Doccil, Jesse 58
Dollison, Eliz. 30
John 30

Dolzall, John 28
Donaldson, Elizabeth 24
Donehow, Sumerset 30
Donty, Benjamin 20
Doyal, James 17
Doyall, James 51
Dowey, Jas. 66
Robert 73
Dowlass, William 26
Drew, Deliah 57
John 57
Drewry, Morgan 36
Dreyers, William 45
Driggers, William 10
Dry, William 8, 16
DuBois (Debois), Jane 2
John 2, 34, 55
Dugers (Drugers?), Thomas 39
Dulony, James 51
Duman, John 48
Dumkin, David 57
Dun, John 63
Robert 63
Dunbar, John 10, 17
Duncan, David 57
James 55
Dunham, William R. 71
W. R. 73
Dunn, Elizabeth 8
John 8, 19, 25, 30, 35(2), 58, 59
Mary 58, 59
Richard 8, 21, 35(2), 58, 59
Robert 19, 35(2)
Dunshow, Summersit 40
Dyson, Leonard 63

Easlace, Michael 34
Eason, Benjamin 65
Edge, John 47
Edwards, Alexander 25, 26
Ann 44
Charles 61
Robert 2(2), 4(2), 5(2), 6, 7,
12, 14, 17, 18, 21, 29,
37, 44, 46, 47, 48, 50(2)
Samuel 43
Sarah 43
William 12, 13, 14, 52
Egner, Phillip 33
Elbzey, Meriday 3
Eleheridge (Ethridge), Sam. 20
Elkings, Samuel 73
Ellis, Elenor 65
Elizabeth 1
Evan 64
J. 68
John 63, 64
Wm. 65, 67
Elliss, Esan 16
Evan 18
William 19
Ellzey, Meriday 3
Elwell, Benja. 23, 36, 73
John 23, 56
Richard 56
Elwett, Benjamin 73
Elwill, Richard 56
Encek, William 26
Ennis, Levey 18
Ervin, Jared 61, 63, 69
Erwin, James 15
Etheridge, Ann 16
Samuel 16
Ethridge, Ann 16
Saml. 11, 16, 20
Evans, Elizabeth 61
Jno. 35
Jonath. 25
Peter 3
Thomas 3

Fairley (Zuilley?), John 22
Faulk, John 66

Jonathan 65
Richard 65
Simon 65
Faulks, John 61
Fault, Richard 65
Simon 65
Felveg(?), John 37
Penney, Thomas 23
Fester, Stephen 62
Field, Thomas 30
Filby, Joseph 14
Finkley, Charles 54
Fitz Gerrald, Thos. 62
Fitzgearreld, Thos. 62
Fitzrandolph, Benjamin 1, 15,
18, 29, 50, 73
  Edward 34
  Elizabeth 50
  Mary 50
Fivash, John 4
Fiverash, John 4
Flear, Stephen 6
Fleater, Betty 8
Flowers, Edward 6, 25, 27, 28,
29, 54, 55, 56
  Ignatias (Ignatius) 16, 49, 50
  John 27, 28, 29
  Uriah 72
Fokes, John 66
  Josiah 66
  Wm. 66
Forbes, Wm. 35
Forester, John 39, 48
Fort, Elias 10, 14
  Joseph 3, 10, 14(2), 22(2),
23(2), 29, 33, 43, 45,
48, 53
  Nancy 12
Francis, Robert 42
French (Trench?), Richard 52
Fuller, Benja. 39
Funt, 38

Gardner, John 2
Garlington, Christopher 5
Garvan, Mathew 6
Carven, John 66(2)
Gaurier, Joseph R. 68
Gautier, Joseph Richd. 65
  J. R. 68
  Thomas Nicholas 69
Gauture, J. R. 68
Gerves, John 17
Gervis, John 5, 36
Gibbs, George 42, 43
Gibson, John 15
  Jordan 10
  Walter (Waltar) 1, 38, 49, 55,
56, 63, 66
  William 38
Gifford, Henry 25
Gilchrist, John 22(2), 23, 31,
37, 52, 53
Gill, John 37
Glair, Stephen 56
Glass, Levi 44
Goadon, Joseph 13
Goadson, William 14
Godwin, David 48, 49, 50, 58
  Simon 67
  Stephen 72
Golly, Anthony 27, 30, 35
Gooden, Daniel 73
Gooding, Christofer 64
Goodwin, Christopher 53
  David 42, 58
Gordon, James 45
Gotier, Joseph Richard 64
Graedy, John 28
Graham, Alexander 52, 60
  Andrew 4, 7, 17, 52
  Gray 7
  Henry Hale 25
Grahm., Thos. 42

Grainger, John 47
Grange, Jno. 26, 64
  John P. 64
Granham, Caleb 62
Grant, Alexander 30
Grantham, Edward 49
  James 40, 42
  John 33
  Richard 33, 51
  William 29, 33
Graves, Sarah 40
Gray, Agnes 7
  Alexander 53
  Elizabeth 7
  Margaret 36
  Mary 7
  Neil 19
  Neill 7(2)
  Will 8, 52
  William 6, 7(4), 11, 19, 36,
52, 66
Green, Amy 31
  John 31, 38, 60
  Robert 31, 61
  Simon 38
  William 38, 56
Greer, Robert 12
  Thomas 32
Gregory, Alex. 58
  W. 24
Grey, William 66
Grice, Mary 37
  Moses 37
Griffeth, Thomas 24
Grimes, Willis 11
Gromes(?), Grimes(?) 31
Groves, Sarah 62
Gullage, William 44
Gulledge, Jeremiah 13
  William 37
Guyton, Jacob 60

Hadson, John 47
Hailey, Edward 17
Haines, Samuel 13, 15, 17
Hales, Saml. 66
Hall, Ann 52
  Enoch 5(2), 52
  Jno. 65
  Lewis 51(2), 52
  Susannah 51
  Thomas 27, 30, 35(2)
  William 51(2)
Halleor, Richard 35
Halt, Thomas 35
Hamilton, Esther 15
Hammon, John 49
Hammond, John 14
Hanchey, Jacob 69
Hanell, George 43
Hardwick, Sinrill 1
Hargrove, Brittian 73(2)
Harnett, Cornelius 20
  Mary 16
Harnicks, Jno. 29
Harriet, John Foreman 34
Harrison, Edward 8
  John 60
  Richard 44
Harvey, Alexander 1, 2, 28, 33
  A. 31
  T. W. 72
Hassel, Jas. 65
Hassell, Jas. 21, 38
Hatcher, Isaac 40
  Isam 19, 40
  Mary 19
Haw, A. 68
Hawksworth, William 24
Hays, Joshua 16, 20, 25
Hayne, Elizabeth 69
  Thomas 69
Haynes, Margaret 2
  Rodger 2

Roger 2, 27
Hays, Joshua 25
  Luther 25
Hayse, Joshua 1
Hellur, Richard 28, 29, 36
Helpburn, Charles 3, 4
Henderson, Richard 27, 30, 31
  Thomas 19, 27
  William 70(2)
Hendon, Josiah 20, 25, 33
  Isham 15, 33
  William 13, 33
Henly, Peter 2
Herbird, William 37
Herell, Elisha 61
Herrin, Enoch 65
Hester, John 67
  Stephen 15, 63
  Thomas 15, 42, 52
  William 52, 57(2), 67
Hill, Abraham 45
  Abram 45
  Isaac 9
  John 45, 57
  Micajah 63
  Phillip 66
Hinnant, John 65
Hofmillon, Alexr. 41
Hogg, James 64
  Robert 64
Hollaman, James 65
Holleman, Howell 32
Hollen, James 15
Hollingsworth, John 21
  Mary 4, 5, 30
  Samuel 21, 30, 31
  Stephen 4, 5, 8, 17, 21, 30
  Valentine 4, 5, 30
Holmes, Moses 61
  William 5
Holms, Gabrel 73
  Richard 73(2)
Holt, William 26
Holton, John 32
Hooper, A. M. 72
Horn, Jane 49, 50
  Nathan 28, 32, 54, 61
  Thomas 40
  William 18, 49, 50, 62
How, Arthur 6
  William 5
Howard, Benjamin 27
  Hezekiah 27
  John 22
  Joseph 27, 38
  M. 3, 13
  Sarah 38
  William 38, 43
Howe, A. 10, 11, 12, 14, 19, 51
  Arthur 2, 3, 4, 8, 9, 11, 14,
18, 26, 35(2)
  Robert 9
  William 40, 42
Hows, A. 7
Hudson, Elizabeth 58
Hufham, Jno. 67
Hughes, Edward 39
Humphres, Benja. 38
Humphrey, Benja. 24, 49, 55, 56
  Chembers 45
  Joseph 55, 56
Humphreys, Benjamin 1, 38
  Chambers 48
Hunt, Cresswell 38
Hursett(?), Lewis 21
Husk, John 64
Huske, John 64

Ichner, Catherine 32
  Phillip 32
Ikner, Catherine 33
  George 30, 36, 40, 41
  Michael 40
  Philip 14

Phillip 30, 40, 58
Ingmore(?), John 55
Inman, Eliz. 6, 51
  James 6, 25, 51
Irvin, Nicholas 46
Isham, Jas. 60
Ivekner, Phillip 37
Ivey, Adam 30, 53
  James 10
  Rubin 11
  Thomas 14, 27, 28, 56

Jackson, James 35(2)
  John 39
  Marsha 35
  Thomas 11
James, Soloman 3
Jessfield, John 26
Jillisey(?), Meadows 31
Johnson, Elizabeth 34
  Jacob 67
  James 34, 67
  Joshua 67
  Margaret 67
  Nehemiah 58
  Peng(?) 69
  Robert 2, 3(2)
  Saml. 67
  Solomon 9
  Thos. 61
  William 5, 34, 67
Johnston, A. 73
  Amos 73
  Enoch 67
  Gabriel 4, 5, 16, 20, 42, 55
  James 28, 31, 32, 45(2), 47, 56
  Jacob 67(2)
  Jesse 73
  Joel 68
  John 23
  John Jr. 30
  Joshua 67
  Margaret 67
  Peregrine 18, 19
  Perygreen 18, 19
  Rob. 49
  Robert 11, 53
  Saml. 30, 50(2), 67
  Solomon 9, 10, 12, 13, 33(2), 36, 45, 53
  Solomon Jr. 14
  Solomon Sr. 14, 37
  Judge 57
Jones, Ann 34, 55
  Charity 12
  Edward 9, 25(2), 26, 27, 28, 63, 65
  Frederick 16
  Griffith 3, 26
  Hannah 28
  Hezekiah 66
  Isaac 9, 24, 25(2), 26, 31, 69, 71
  James 67
  John 2, 11, 12, 34(2), 35, 37, 55
  Marmadrake 30
  Musgrove 71
  Nathan 43
  Thomas 25, 43
  William 63, 64

Kally, Mathew 58
Karon, Robert 58
Keel, Caleb 19
Keller, George 4
Kelling, George 4
Kelly, James 68
  J. 72
  John 38, 73
  Mary 72
  Matthew 1, 60, 68
Kelsoe, Alexr. 69

Kemp, D. W. 72
  John 67
  Joseph 2, 67, 68
Kenady, Isaac 36
Kenedy, Samuel 41
Kersey, Thomas 8, 33, 53
Kessak, Archibald 10 (see McKessack)
King, Jane 22
  John 22, 39, 48, 53, 60
  Michael 66
Kinlow, Thomas 54
Klimum, Gideon 46
Knox, John 29

Laconstadt, Ereck(?) 65
Laird, Murd. 46
Lamb, Abraham 13, 54
  Isaac 13, 50, 54
  Joshua 5
  Thomas 11, 51
Lambert, John 56
Lansdell, John 71
Larkins, John 27
  William 27
Lee, Joshua 62, 66
  Joshua Jr. 66
  Stephen 66
Legate, John 14
Leger, Andrew 2
Legere, Andrew 2
Leget, Absalom 41
  John 19, 23, 36
Legett, Absalom 36, 37
  John 7, 14, 19, 23(2), 33, 35(2), 36, 37, 41, 44, 45, 51, 55, 56, 57
  Rachel 35
Legg, Alexander 32, 56
Legget, John 41, 52
Leggett, John 36, 37, 40
Legit, John 33
Lemon, Angus 68
Lennen, Morgan 15
Lennon, Dennis 4, 6, 72
  Experience 6
  George 72
  Jno. 26
  John 26, 62
  Moore 72
Leonard, Jacob 70
  John 34
  Judge 4
  Thos. 34
Leweas, John 25
  Hanson 16
  J. 67, 72
  James 11, 38, 58(2)
  Josiah, Jr. 5, 21, 58(2)
  Richard 62
  Richard Mallington 8, 70
  Saml. 17
  Sarah 59
  Solomon 16, 67
  William 16, 20, 27
Liews, James 38
Ligett, John 6
Likes, Jacob 46
Linscom, John 8(2), 21
Linscombe, John 23
Littel, Mary 48
  Thos. 48
  William 48
Little, Archibald 41, 45
  Jesse 49
  Joseph 49
  Thomas 45(2), 46, 48, 49
Lloyd, Ann 66
  David 25, 26, 66
Lock, David 16
  Elizabeth 28
  John 28
  Joseph
  Leonard 36

Mary 25
  Thomas 28, 36
Locks, Joseph 6
Lockwood, John 29
Logartie, Edmond 30
Logatie, Edmund 27
Lord, Peter 3, 12
  William 30
Lordy, John 55
Lowery, James 22(2), 31, 50
  William 50
Lowerys, James 19
Loyd, Ann 66
  David L. 25, 26, 66
Lucas, Elizabeth 39
  Francis 39, 43
  John 38, 43
Lucas, John 43
Lyon, Elizabeth 39
  George 39, 44
  James 30, 39
  John 21
  Mildred 21

McAlister, Alexr. 21
McAllister, Danl. 68
  William 15
McArthur, John 52
  Neill 52
  Peter 52
McCarnag, John 38
McCauslin, John 40
McClaine, A. 47
  Hugh 53
McClaren, Arch. 4, 5
McClouskey, Neill 55
McCoalskey, Archd. 44
McConkey, Robert 44
McConley, Alexander 5
McCordsby(?), Duncan 73
McCoulsky, Duncan 73
  Neill 16
McCraine, John 53
McCrainey, John 10, 23(2), 37, 51
McCramey, Gilbert 51
McCrane, Hugh 39
  John 44
McCraney, John 37, 45
McCrary, John 45
McCruney, John 19
McDaniel, Agnes 34
  Alexander 31, 47, 56
  Archibold 36, 60
  Daniel 44
  James 6, 7, 11, 15, 17, 18, 34, 35, 36, 52
  John 52, 60
McDuffee, Dougald 40
  John 40
McDuffie, Neele 21
McEacham, Archd. 46
McEacharn, Donald 41
McEachern, Archd. 41, 55, 56
  David 41
McEachers, Archd. 41
McEwen, John 70
  W. M. 71
McFall, Malcom 45
  Neill 29, 39
McFallaw, Dannel 45
McFater, Malcom 37
McFatter, Alexr. 72
McFee, Sarah 21
McFoal, Neal 41
McGee, Elias 71(2)
McGees, Malley 56
McGill, Archd. 42, 52
  Roger 37
McKay, Alexander 3(2), 20
  Archibald 68
  Daniel 73
  Ever 20
  Iver 20, 21

J. 68
Jane 3, 21
John 30, 46, 60, 64, 66, 68,
    71
Margaret 20
Neill 3
McKee, Wm. 69, 71
McKeithan, Alexander 16
  Daniel 40
  Donald 29
  Duncan 16, 29, 40
  Gillr. 40
  Isabella 29
McKeller, Peter 45
McKenne(?), John 64
McKimrie, John 65
McKinne, John 69
McKinzie, William ?
McKissack (McKissak, McKizsak),
    Archibald 8, 9, 10,
    11, 14, 17, 20, 26,
    38, 44, 47, 51(2), 58
McKoulikely, Jas. 66
McKuthan, Alexn. 21
McLauchlan, Donald 41
McLauchlin, Jan 41
McLaughlin, Daniel 22, 29, 41
McLaughlin, John 57
McLaughling, John 13
  Mary 13
McLean, Alexander 54
  Daniel 11
  Donald 4
  Hector 38
  John 10, 14
McMath, John 6, 7, 58
McMillan, Dugald 37, 56
  Iver 16
  John 37
McMulon, Ever 44
McMuth, John 32
McNabb, James 44, 58
McNair, John 55
McNaughton, Charles 60
  John 72
  Neill 16
McNeal, Hector 39
McNear, Daniel 37
  John 37
McNeil, Neil 3, 10, 12
McNeill, Daniel 55
  Hector 37, 39, 44, 45, 47, 48,
      56, 57
  James 55
  John 55
  Malcolm 41
  Neil(1) 29, 57
  Turkel 10(2)
  William 14, 55
McNichols, Sarah 66
McNiel, Hector 14, 28
  William 16
McNorton, Neill 60
McNull (McNeill?), William 55
McNutt (McNull?), Wm. 40
McPhoal, John 8
McPoumecy, An 39
McRa, Murdock 45, 56
McRae, Murdock 58
  Wm. 8, 18
McRee, J. 64
  Jane 50
  Robt. 33, 50, 63
  Saml. 26
  William 21, 24, 29, 34, 38,
      53(2), 57, 63
McWhorter, John 26

M____, William 38
MacAllister, Danl. 68
MacLain, A. 9
  Archibald 2
MacMillan, John 68
Macon, James 2

Macree, Murd. 57
Magee, Mary 15
Makay, Alexr. 39
Malky, Eliz. 24
  Jonathan 24
Mallington, Richard 8, 18, 27,
    38, 40, 55
Malsby, John 34
Maluine, A. 22
Manning, Ephriam 29
Marsden, Richard 2
Marshall, James 45
  John 2
Martin, George 9, 27, 30, 35(2)
  Joseph 50
Mason, William 12, 35
Massey, Joseph 10
Maulsby, John 34
  Mary 34
  Wm. 7, 30, 34, 35
Maultsby, James 57
  John 57
Maxwell, Elisha 27
Meacham, Thomas 33
Mears, James 67
  Jona. 67
Meekes, Francis 68
Melton (Milton), Joseph 48
  Lusee 48
Melvin, Daniel 4, 6, 27, 70
  John 70
Mercer, Joseph 12, 21, 22, 44
  Joshua 17
  Maluchi 21
  Nour 21
  Solomon 21, 22
Meredath, Elizabeth 69
  Elizar 17
  Hannah 69
  James 69(2)
  John 69(2)
  Malachi 22
  Nathan 69
  Wm. Haw 69
Meredith, Elennor 69
  Jane 69
  Joseph 69
Messar, Henry 12, 33, 46
Messer, Henry 40, 46, 57
  Joseph 21
  Solomon 49
Milars, Ralph 42
Millan, Christian 31
Miller, Ralph 35(2), 42, 64, 66
Milton (Melton), Joseph 48
Mims, David 31
  Grace 31, 46
  Thomas 31, 46, 69(2)
Mitchell, Anthy. 31
Monroe, Hugh 21
Moody, Daniel 10, 13
Moor, Benjamin 63
Moore, A. 1, 52, 53, 54, 55,
    56, 59
  Alfred 17, 36, 37, 38, 39,
      40, 41, 42, 43, 44,
      45, 46, 47, 48, 49,
      50, 51, 52, 53, 54,
      56, 57, 58
  Ann 20
  Barringer 24
  Benjamin 24, 27(2)
  Jean 48
  M. 15, 30, 31, 34, 47, 48, 49
  Mary 19, 24
  Maurice 3, 4, 20, 30
  Roger 30
  Thomas 12
  William 8, 16, 17, 35, 53, 54
Moorehead, James 22, 39, 48, 53,
    70
  Jane 39
  William 22, 47, 48
  Sarah 48

Moory, Wm. 47
Morgan, Goen 14, 31, 45
  Green 45
  Wallar(?) 65
  Waltar 67
  William 67
Morley, Amile 1
  David 3, 21, 36
Morpe, Elisha 73
Morrison, Duncan 1
Mosley, Thomas 9
Mouat, William 11
Mulford, Ephraim 14
  Thos. 66
Mulkey, Elizabeth 19
  Jonathan 19
Mullington (Mallington), Richard
    3, 5(2), 14, 27
Munroe, Lewis 32
Muns, Lewis 57
Munse, Lewis 58
Murfey, Neill 45
Murphy, Hugh 66, 69, 71(4)
  Robert 72
Musselwhite, Thomas 10

Neale, Samuel 47
  Thos. 64
Neil, Samuel 47
Nelson, James 62
Nessfield, Ann 26
  John 2, 3, 26, 27
Newberry, Jesse 17
  John 1, ?, 11
Newburry, Jesse 7
  John Jr. 6, 7
  Mary 6
Newbury, Deborah 31
  Jesse 11, 17, 19, 31, 35
  John 17, 19
  Mary 19
  William 36
Nichols, Coleman 41, 49, 50, 58
  Martha 58
Nickels, Coleman 62
Nickles, Coleman 67
  Ephraim 67
Nixon, John 17
Norton, Daniel 13, 14, 55
  Jacob 16, 20, 55
  Thomas 13, 55
  William Jr. 16, 20
  William Sr. 13, 14, 55
Nuten, Patrick 43
Nuton, Patrick 43

Oates, Caroway 44
  Carraway 29
  Connoway 33
  Jethro 49, 50
  Joseph 18, 29, 33, 46, 68
Oats, Joseph 69(2)
Oberry (Obery, Obeny), Henry 13,
    14, 23, 33, 53(2)
  James 33, 53
Obyans, Timothy 49
Odam, Thomas 11
Odom, Aaron 11, 15, 17, 24
  Abram 47
  Aron 56
  Ben 31, 32
  Benjamin 31, 32, 46, 47(2), 48
  Isaac 15, 17, 32
  James 13
  John 11, 17, 53
  Thamar 47
  Thomas 15, 17, 47, 58
Odon, Aaron 24
Oliver, William 20
O'Quin, Tarler 45
O'Quinn, Hardy 13
O'Quint, Taler 48
Ornie, Thomas 26
Oveler, Elizabeth 20

John 20, 24, 28
Overton, Titus 23
Owen, Jno. 12, 30
  John 29
  Thomas 24, 25, 29, 30, 42, 58, 63
  Titus 23
Owens, Ephraum 20
  Thomas 20, 50, 56, 70
Oxendine, Charles 14, 32

Pace, James 13, 14, 53
  Mourning 53
  William 29
Palmer, George 19, 22, 24
  John 47
  Mary Ann 19, 22, 24
  Moses 72
Parker, Francis 38, 73
  Moses 72
  Tabitha 38
  William 61, 62
Parvisal, Isa. 30
Pates, Joseph 68
Patterson, Daniel 48
Paul, Abraham 9, 10, 16, 17
Pekes, Mr____ 20
Pemberton, Edward 57
  James 57
  John 57
  Margaret 57
  Rebecca 57
Pennett (Bennett?), Wm. 66
Perddro, John 25
Perkins, Ann 19, 39, 50
  John 9, 13, 15
Pernell, Cornelious 67
Pervers, ____ 17
Peterson, John 45
Phares, James 48
Philips, M. 68
  Mark 68
Phillips, John 56
Pigott, Nathl. 35
Pike, Samuel 3, 4, 5, 6, 67, 73
Pirkins, Ann 8, 9
Pitman, ____ 6
  Isham 57
  Isom 51
  Jacob 31, 39, 45, 48
  Jesse 13, 14, 27, 28, 32, 51, 57
  Joel 32
  John 29
  Lott 32, 57
  N. Cannah 39
  Rachel 32
  Thomas 51
Plummer, Eliphe 48
  Eliphey 47
  Ellipha 3
  Elliphe 35
  Jeremiah 3, 47, 48
  John 71
  Joseph 3, 12, 35, 47, 48, 71
  Moses 12, 28
  Sarah 3
  Zachariah 71
Pope, Jacob 8, 43
Porter, John 21, 31, 47
Portexsent, Joseph 2
Pouncy, Antho. 47
Powe, Thomas 50
Powel, Isaac 73
Powell, Absolom 62
  Benja. 41
  Isaiah 12, 37
  Restore 46
Poynter, Argulas 71
  Mary Jane 68
Price, John 46
  Joseph 35, 41, 46
Pridgen, Mathew 22
Prince, ____ 25
  Nicholas 46
Prior, Luke 22

Protherough, John 25
Protherow, John 25
Prothrow, Margaret 25
Protrough, John 3
Pryor, Luke 11, 47
Pugh, Hugh 49
  W. 46
Purdie, Jas. 64
  J. S. 67, 68, 69, 70, 71, 72, 73
  James Samuel 71
Purdre, James 64

Quince, Capt. 7
  John 47
  Richard 40, 47

Rabon, Thomas 6, 23
Raburn, Thomas 21
Rae, Catherine 40
  Hugh 40
Raford, Robert 63
Raiford, Robt. 45
Ramsay, Gibbert 56
Randolph, Edward 27, 34
Rawls, Marma. 69
Ray, Dugal 73
  Duncan 72
  Isaac 28
Reaves, Edward 72
  Wm. 72
Reeves, Nathaniel 34
Regan, Joseph 17, 53
Register, William 66
Reynolds, George 12
Rhuark, Samuel 39
Rice, Nathaniel 42, 70
Richardson (Richuson), Amis 65
  Elizabeth 42
  James 23
  John 34
  Nathl. 43, 55
  N. 65
  Sam 25
  Saml. Beall 65
  Samuel 43, 64
  Thos. 63
Robbins, Arthur 57
  Jethro 62
Roberson, Thomas 5
Roberts, James 28
  John 58, 69
  Reuben 17
Robeson, John 2, 63
  Peter 18, 19, 45, 63
  Thomas 4, 5, 9, 16, 18, 19, 25, 26, 27, 29, 30, 34, 35, 42, 45, 48
  Thos. Peter 63
Robinson, Thomas 1, 41
Robison, Bartram 66
  Peter 48
  Thomas 37, 52
Rock, Edmond 36
Rogers, John 9
Rogerson, John 43, 44
Rollin, Arthur 50
Ronald, George 3, 4
Rools, Juren 34
Roos, John 10
Ross, David 27
Rouches, David 53
Rouse, John 14
  Peter 10
Rowan, George 5
  John 4
  Mat 6
  Mathew 6, 16, 21, 49, 73
Rowke, Edmund 27
Rowland, James 14, 32, 54
  John 32, 54
  Thomas 12, 19, 32
Russ, David 1, 24, 27, 49
  Eleazer 66

  Jas. 66
  John 12, 52, 66
  John Jr. 52, 62, 63
  Jonadab 5
  Joseph 66
  Mary 9
  Moses 39
  Thomas 9, 12, 24, 27, 66
  Thomas Jr. 9
  William 52
Russel, Thomas 43
Rutherford, Thomas 12, 13, 24, 28, 30

Sallars, Russ 62
  Wm. 64
Saltar, James 1, 6
  John 49, 56
  Richard 4, 50
  Sarah 1
  William 50
Saltor, William 1
Sanders, Christopher 1(2), 6
  Elcy 1
  Emilia 1
  James 54
  Nathaniel 39, 47
  Sarah 1
  Thomas 1, 66
  William 1
Sapp, William 18, 19
Sattar (see Salter), James 1
  Sarah 1
Sealey, Tobias 41
Sellers, Ann 50
  Benja. 57
  John 70
  Matthew 50
  Simon 50
Schaw, Daniel 72
Scott, Robt. 64, 66
  Thos. 64, 66
Scripps, Jos. 32
Scuister, John 52
Sharp, K. 23
Shaw, Alexander 53
  Anguish 50
  Archd. 40, 53
  John 66
  Neil(1) 44, 53
Shembs, Joseph 7
Shepard, Stephen 35
Shepperd, Stephen 6
Shingleton, Mary 34
  William 34
Shipman, Daniel 1, 59, 60
  James 1(2), 6, 58(2)
Sibbit, Wm. 62
Sike, Isaiah 73
Sikes, Jacob 65
Simpson, Edward 70
  Frederick 68
  Hannah 50
  Jas. 39, 50
  Jno. 57
  John 46(2), 57
  Peter 50
  Thomas 28, 50, 53
Sims, Henry 17, 34, 36(2), 46
  Isaac 20
  James 14, 30, 31
  Margaret 36
  Robert 34, 46
  William 14, 36
Simson, Thomas 28
Sincombs, John 36
Sinkler, John 63
Sinscom, John 8
Skinner, Stephen 34
Slingsby, John 55
Small, John 23
Smalley, Joshua 58
Smith, Archibald 36, 45
  Benjamin 70

Daniel 23, 31, 39, 45, 47
David 30
Henry 33(2)
Jacob 71
James 21, 49, 65, 71
Jno. 66
John 5(2), 12, 14, 19, 21, 31,
   32, 41, 43, 47, 51, 54,
   56, 60, 66, 70(2)
Joseph 9
Lucey(?) 63
Richard 3(2), 8, 9, 11, 13,
   14, 15, 20, 28, 29,
   37, 38, 48, 51, 54,
   55
Samuel 19, 21, 54, 55, 56
Simon 60
Stephen 43
Susanna 54
William 8, 23, 32, 70
Speir, John 49
   Wm. 49
Spiars, Solomon 61
Spiller, J. 67
Stark, John 42, 58
Starkey, John 4
Starlin, Thomas 51
Starling, John 47
Stephe, Barnabas 57
   Joshua 68
Sterling, John 53
Stevans, Eli 66
   Wm. 65, 66
Stevens, Barnabas 15, 21, 49, 57
   Charles 40
   Eli 66
   Isaac 18(2), 19, 69
   Isaar 46
   John 17, 34
   Joshua 41, 42, 69(2)
   Oliver 49
   Sarah 17, 18, 34
   William 58, 61, 66
Stewart, Alexander 14, 21
   Duncan 69
   James 3, 9, 10(3), 11, 12, 14,
      29, 36(2), 42, 55, 69
   Jennet 55
   John 57, 64
   Patrick 16
   Robert 4, 38
   William 13, 55, 71
Stone, Benjamin 27, 34
   William 34
Storey, Patrick 69
Straham, Othniel 38
Strahams, Othiel 22
Strahan, Othneil 43
Straken, Neel 22
   Othniel 27
   Sarah 22
Strawhorn, Cornelius 70
Strickland (Stricklan, Stricklen,
      Stricklin), Abraham
      11, 37, 54
   Martha 37
   Phillip 46
   William 1, 40, 46
Strong, Return(?) 65
Stuart, James 33
   Pat 34
Suister, John 52
Sullivan, Isaac 68
Sutton, Bailey 69
   Baley 67
   Beaman 69, 70
   Christopher 68
   John 68, 72
   Saml. 46
   William 70
Summersett, William 63
Swan, Samuel 49
Swann, John 16
   Samuel 16

Sweat, Robt. 44
Sweeten, Lisha 37
Sweeting, Elish 3
Swindell, Sal. 73
Syniths (Smyth?), James 69

Tadors, Marsh 33
Tail, Jonothan 32
   Thomas 40
Tarliff, Moses 47
Tayler, John Lewis 65
Taylor, Archibald 53
   Lewis 69
   Josiah 18, 32, 33
   William 32
Tenny, Thomas 48
Terrill(?), Robert 8(2)
Terry, John 15
Thembe, Joseph 6
Thembs, Cornelius 19
Thomas, Benjamin 20, 28, 29
   Evan 20, 29, 30
   George 4, 64, 66(2)
   Henry 72
   Jane 72
   Jonathan 70, 72
   Lewis 54
   Michael 72
   Richard 29
Thombs, Joseph 7
Thompson, Charles 16
   William 47
Thomson, Chaves 54
   William 58
Thornont, Samuel 54
Thornton, Samuel 15, 25, 42, 54
Thumbs, Joseph 34
   Thomas 19, 35(2)
Tiler, Needham 22
Tilman, Gideon 1, 18
Toller (Toler), William 45
Tommy, Henry 56
Toreman, Harriet 34
   John 34
Torster, John 22
Treadwell, John 72
Trench (French?), Richard 52
Trowel, James 10
Trowell, James 9
Trueblood, Aless. 6
Tryon, Gov. 57, 58
   William 18, 19
Turner, Daniel 70
   John 43, 51, 73
   Lazarus 70
Tuts, Joseph 19
Tyler, Moses 11, 22
   Nedam 11
   Needham 22

Upton, James 14
   Robert 52

Valentine, Harey 67
Vance, Thos. 35
Varnans (Vernon?), Ephraim 63
Vernon, Ann 42
   Ephraim 63
Vernor, Robert 32

Waddell, John 66
Waddle, Hugh 22, 73
Waid, Reuben 26(2)
Waide, Wm. 69
Walker, John 19, 22, 24
Walsh, John 32
Waltham, James 40
Walton, James 40
Ward, Philip 67
   William 66
Watson, John 37
   William James 64
Wayne, Gabriel 28
Weatherly, Cade 66

Weathersby, Isam 72
Weir, Emiston 23
Wen, John
Werrell, Benj. 66
West, James 47, 65
   Willis 72
Wistfield, Sarah 58
White, Ann 52
   David 15, 57
   David Lindsay 28, 53, 55, 56
   David Lenzy 33
   Ganel 26
   George 70
   Griffith 28, 33
   Griffith Jones 33
   James (Sheriff) 1, 6, 8, 12,
      19, 22, 23, 24(2), 28,
      30, 38, 42, 51, 53, 55,
      56, 64
   J. 69
   Jane Kemp 2
   Jno. 56
   John 1(3), 2(2), 19, 28, 31,
      33, 49, 54, 55, 69(2)
   Joseph 34, 52
   Luke 70
   M. R. 72
   Mary 2, 19, 52
   Mathew R. 72
   Peter 25
   Robert 2
   Stephen 29, 54, 71
   Thomas 3, 5, 40
   William 2, 21, 26, 27, 30,
      35(2), 71
Wilkerson, James 4, 9, 10
   Philip 15
   William 4, 9, 10, 16, 73
Wilkes, Isaac 41
   Isack 19
Wilkeson, Archibald 55
   James 16, 38
   John 13, 18
   Mary Ann 18
   Philip 18, 19, 48
   Philip Jr. 18
   William 18, 73
Wilkinson, Wm. 11, 13
Wilkison, Richard 36
Will, John 57
Williams, Herkey 23
   Hickey 15
   Joseph 43, 45, 48, 49
   Martha 48
   Suck 65
   Wm. 65
Williamson, Lewis 62
Williford, Jordan 72
Willis, Betty 57
   Dan. 50
   Daniel 5(2), 6(2), 12, 13,
      14(2), 26, 28, 29, 30,
      32(3), 57
   Danl. 50, 52, 53, 54
   Eliz. 57
   George 12, 32, 52
   Jeremiah 61
   John 40
Wills, John 18(2), 19
Wilson, Edward 61
   John 8, 36, 57, 58
   Josiah 27
   Laban 72
   Louis 72
   Rebecca 36
   Richard 72
   Robert 36
   Silvanus 23(3), 35(2), 36(3)
      46
   Sylvanus 46
Wingate (Whingate), John 57(3)
Win, George 65
Wir, Edminston 11, 35
Wire, Edminston 35

Wise, Robert 27
Wood, Is. 58
  Lucy 48
  Philip (Phillip) 8, 48
  Sampson 26, 48
Woodard, Benj. 60
Woolf, Isaac 38
Wootan, John 10
Worth, John 15, 16, 18

Yarbrough, James 22
  John 22
Yates, John 49, 64, 69
Yeates, John 42
Young, David 41, 56
  George 42, 44
  Levi 17
  Lucy 52
  James 56
  Ralph Ben 42

Zaird (Laird?), Murd. 46
Zuilley, John 22

www.ingramcontent.com/pod-product-compliance
Lightning Source LLC
Chambersburg PA
CBHW020702300426
44112CB00007B/478